BEYOND THE BAT

SECRETS OF A SUPERHERO SCRIBE

STAN BERKOWITZ

ILLUSTRATIONS BY DAN RIBA

Copyright © 2024 Stanley Berkowitz
All Rights Reserved

No part of this book may be reproduced in any form or by any electronic or mechanical means, including information storage and retrieval systems, without written permission from the author, except for the use of brief quotations in a book review.

ISBN: 979-8-3340-5385-4

Author photo by Teagan Clive
Illustrator photo by Colin Riba

For Teagan

CONTENTS

INTRODUCTION _____9

This book isn't an autobiography. It's a series of essays about the craft and business of storytelling. So you don't need to read it in order. You don't even need to read these contents in order.

CHAPTER ONE: HOW TO WIN AN EMMY _____13

Passing a professional milestone can open one's eyes to personal milestones that have already been passed.

CHAPTER TWO: WRITTEN BY STAN BERKOWITZ… AND GOD: Animating the Bible _____25

A newcomer to the Old Testament wonders if there could have been a contemporary-style writers' room 2500 years ago.

CHAPTER THREE: THE GREEN GROUP _____43

An incident in first grade leads to a career-long obsession with superhero vigilantes

CHAPTER FOUR: WHEN THINGS GO WELL… THERE'S SELDOM A STORY TO TELL _____53

An easy delivery for an animated Superman leads to an underperforming adolescence, while Spider-Man is nearly still-born… despite Stan Lee serving as midwife.

CHAPTER FIVE: NOTES ON NOTES _____69

*Sometimes notes can help a writer.
Or they can ruin everything.*

CHAPTER SIX: SUPERHEROES GROW UP... BUT SHOULD THEY? _____ 85

A drug-addled prop man's big green rubber phallus provokes questions about who we're writing for.

CHAPTER SEVEN: "DAMMIT, HOOKER, SHE WAS MY NIECE!" _____ 101

An episodic script's shape-changing odyssey from outline to airtime.

CHAPTER EIGHT: RACISM AND ME _____ 117

If you're a racist, can you make a good movie? Or even be a stand-up guy who pays his bills on time? No spoiler alert needed.

CHAPTER NINE: THE HALF-MILLION-DOLLAR BOWL OF SOUP _____ 129

How an attempt at inclusion and diversity in animation led to a Republican version of a fatwa... and an actual one, too!

CHAPTER TEN: SAYING SOMETHING _____ 141

Everyone starts as an amateur. Then comes money. This one's about a young writer's slow march toward professionalism, with detours involving bestiality and gay porn.

CHAPTER ELEVEN: PLAYING THE ODDS ____ 167

What happens after film school if Hollywood never takes your calls? Is it a matter of blind luck? Or are you doing something wrong?

CHAPTER TWELVE: THE ROBIN PROBLEM ___ 181

A tale of a stage show that never should have been.

CHAPTER THIRTEEN: REGRETS _____ 193

An Old Pro has a chance to get back in the action, but will his ego and self-doubt ruin his show... and his own sterling reputation?

CHRONOLOGY _____ 213

The final chapter, a seventy-year timeline that puts everything that's gone before into neat chronological order. For readers who don't believe that time is relative.

ACKNOWLEDGMENTS _____ 223

ABOUT THE AUTHOR _____ 225

ABOUT THE ILLUSTRATOR _____ 227

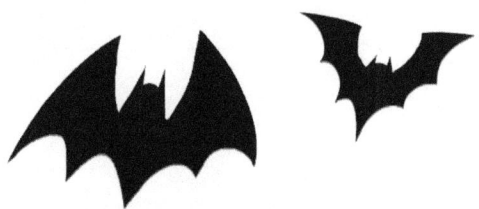

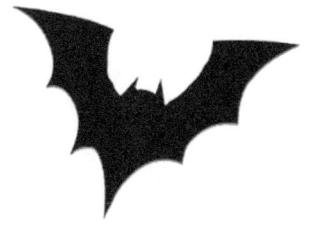

INTRODUCTION

Years ago I co-authored a book called *The Movie Business: A Primer,* which was loosely based on some *Los Angeles Times* articles about how movies get made. I started working on the book with the hope that it would appeal not just to readers who wanted to know more about that specific subject, but also to people who had a general interest in the way things worked. People like my father, who'd go to Disneyland with his family not so much to be awed by the show, but to see *how* the show was made. He was fascinated by the behind-the-scenes stuff, like the way the submarines moved on underwater tracks or how Tinker Bell "flew" on nearly invisible wires. Readers like him, I thought, might be curious to know how studios decided which scripts to produce, how production costs were recouped, and even things like what a "best boy" was.

STAN BERKOWITZ

My co-author David Lees and I worked hard to supply behind-the-scenes movie business info, but once the book came out, we heard from an unexpected contingent: people who were trying to decide if they should go to film school.

Because of readers like them, I've written a cautionary chapter called *Playing the Odds* about a friend I'm calling "Lucky." You often hear about the flukes that allow film students to get into the business, but you seldom hear what happens to the ones who never catch a break, and I think at least one of those stories needed to be told, as discouraging as it might be.

But please don't construe that chapter as an argument against film school. Legitimate educational institutions make it very clear they can't guarantee anything in the way of a career. There are too many aspirants and too few job openings. But if you're passionate enough about getting into show business, things like bad odds aren't going to stop you. Nor will Lucky's story. But I needed to give fair warning about what could happen.

I used the term "film" school, but hardly anyone uses actual, physical film anymore. It's gone the way of slide rules and video tape. But everyone—*everyone*—tells stories, and that's what this book is about: experiences I've had that pertain to both the craft and business of storytelling. It's set mostly in the world of superhero TV animation, because that's where the bulk of my experience has been, but I hope that whatever lessons that might be drawn from these stories can be transposed to almost any medium. I'm also hoping these chapters will be examples of compelling storytelling themselves.

You'll see that most of the lessons involve bad things happening: producers cheating writers and actors, bitter power struggles, old writers flaming out at the ends of their careers, young writers' hopes and dreams savagely crushed. My reason for including so much heartache is that I've found lessons don't come cheap, and little is learned when luck happens to make everything go your way.

If you'd like some proof of that, take a look at the first half of the *When Things Go Well...* chapter. It begins at Warner Bros Animation in the mid-1990s, when I was fortunate enough to step into an operation that had already gotten rid of most of its bugs (except Bugs Bunny, of course), and which was then a smoothly running entity controlled by a wise executive. Where's the drama in that? There wasn't much, nor is there much drama in that half of the chapter; it's simply an argument for centralization of power (and also, for wise executives).

The other half of that chapter makes much the same argument, but from a very different angle: it shows what can happen when power isn't centralized, and everyone is fighting for influence. I'll leave it for you to decide which half of the chapter makes for more compelling reading.

Something else you'll notice as you go through these chapters is that I leave out a lot of names. I do this not to protect anyone, but rather, because when I read other writers' stuff, I tend to get lost if I'm presented with too many names. Often, I'll have to go back to the introductory paragraphs to see which name is associated with which function. So, in many cases, I've cut out the names, and instead referred to people by their function, as in, "the director," "the supervising producer," "the Old Pro," etc. Since this book is more about procedure than personality, I feel comfortable doing this. And trust me, none of the names I've omitted are familiar to the general public. If someone's name happens to be well-known—Stan Lee, William Shatner, Mickey Spillane, etc.—I've left it in.

This book will jump around in time. It's not my autobiography, it's a series of lessons I've learned, so chronology isn't nearly as important as content. For those who can't forsake chronology, I've included a timeline at the end that will indicate where everything fits. For everyone else, feel free to start reading anywhere you'd like.

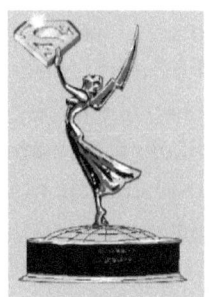

CHAPTER ONE
HOW TO WIN AN EMMY

If you're wondering what it feels like to get one of those statuettes, I'll tell you: it's surreal! Just kidding; I hate that word. Fond as I am of Dali, Magritte et al, I have to admit the word has been drastically overused these last few years. It's been unthinkingly uttered to describe anything from a peculiar cloud formation to the loss of a pet. A more appropriate word in most cases would be "unreal"—something you didn't think was possible, yet happened anyway. And that's exactly how winning felt to me one night in 1998 at Los Angeles's Century Plaza Hotel. I'd spent the previous thirty years writing things no one would have ever considered award-worthy: cop shows mostly, along with some low-budget movies that nobody saw (but if they had been seen, they would have made me seem even less likely to win any kind of award). And then there were my student films. They're described in detail in the *Saying Something* chapter, but suffice it to say, they were far from the positive, life-affirming material that tends to win prizes in Hollywood.

So, sitting with my colleagues that night in the hotel's ballroom, I wasn't sure I'd heard correctly when *The New Batman/Superman Adventures* was called. No one else seemed sure either, and it felt like quite a long time before anyone stood up. But of course, it didn't take long at all—no more than a second or two, and then a dozen of us were up and moving toward the stage.

One of us gave the kind of thank-you speech you've heard a million times, then a hostess led us backstage. There was a small room there which seemed even smaller because it was crowded with scores of Emmy statuettes. As another hostess checked off our names, we were told to take one of the statuettes—any one of them. None had names on them, nor could they, because only a few people at the Academy knew who the winners would be until that moment. So the black plastic strips around the bases of the statuettes were all blank, and it wouldn't be until a few weeks later that the mail would bring us replacement strips with our names, the name of the show, its category, and the date on them. For tonight though, the statuettes would be nameless and interchangeable.

Surprisingly, the statuettes don't come in a box or with any kind of wrapping. You grab it by its waist, go back to your dinner table, set it down in front of you, then wait for the show to end. After that, you walk out through the hotel lobby and wait for your car, your Emmy in hand all the while.

Once I got home, I put the Emmy on top of a kitchen island we'd just bought. The effect was, dare I say it, unreal. It just didn't seem to belong there. Or anywhere else in a place where I lived.

When I started at Warner Bros Animation in 1996, it seemed as though everyone there had at least one, and some more than one. Way more. These awards had helped shine a light on an old Warner Brothers division that had gotten a new lease on life in the late 1980s. Warners characters like Bugs Bunny, Daffy Duck, Sylvester and Tweety had been around since the 1940s, but Warners's new characters – the Animaniacs, Pinky and the Brain and others – had no such history, yet they were expected to go toe-to-toe with the Disney dreadnaught. So a little gold from the TV Academy almost immediately established the new shows' credibility. But all that stuff you've heard about how "the real honor is just being nominated" is flat-out wrong. Nominations are the result of a lot of politicking and hard work—and not just the kind of hard work that goes into making a TV show.

The first step toward getting a nomination is deciding whether you want one or not. And you do have to make that decision, because nominations don't just drop out of the sky, as the uninitiated might assume. Once you decide you want an Emmy, the next step is to choose a category. Some of the choices are easy: is your project a ninety-minute special? A series? Live action or animated? An hour? Half an hour? 15 minutes? Did it premiere in daytime or at night? Those are the easy questions, but some choices aren't so simple. For example, both Emmys I have are for something called "Special Class Animation," and to this day, I cannot tell you precisely what differentiates that class from the regular animation class. My guess is that there were so many entrants in the regular class, which was mostly children's shows, the Academy decided to open a "special" class which might—or might not—have been set up for animated shows that were designed for a slightly older audience. It was totally up to executives at Warners Animation to decide which category to enter our show in, and the executives chose well.

Once the Academy certifies entrants as being eligible to compete in their categories, a list of all the potential nominees is sent out to the members of that branch of the academy (in my case, the Animation branch), and we choose a handful of these shows to become the nominees. This is where nominations begin to seem less like an honor, and more like the result of something similar to a political campaign. That's because it's now a matter of pulling in votes, and the best way a studio can do that is by making sure lots of its employees are voting members of the TV Academy.

So, just before Emmy season, the employees who are members ask those who aren't if they'd like to be. The requirements of Academy membership are not especially onerous: you need to have a job covered by the branch you want to be in, you need to be willing to pay nominal dues every year and you need a couple of Academy members to put their names on your application. Once you're in the Academy, you get a vote in determining who the nominees will be. You even get to vote for your own show if you want, and who wouldn't? Thus, productions from big studios with lots Academy members naturally have a better chance of getting nominated than shows from smaller studios with fewer Academy members.

Once your show is nominated, take a quick look at your competition. You'll know right away who's going to win. That's how it worked for me, anyway. At the time -- the late '90s -- animation was still considered kids' stuff, but it was being judged by adults, of course, so a wink or two at an older audience – a joke that might sail over the kids' heads but hit home with adults, or maybe a reference to something too far in the past for kids to know about -- these things stood out, and not just to the Emmy judges, but also to amateur handicappers like myself.

In 1997, the show I was writing for, *Superman*, was nominated, and one of the competing shows was *Freakazoid*—also from Warners Animation, and a very smart, very funny show. "That'll win," I thought as soon as the nominees were announced, but then I spent weeks trying to convince myself that *Superman* could somehow win. It didn't. *Freakazoid* won that year.

Superman, and most of Warners's other superhero shows of that era, were designed so that adults could watch them with their kids and not have their intelligence insulted. But the scripts never winked at adults, nor was there any material designed exclusively for them. So the shows had an earnestness to them, and that made it tough to compete with the better comedies.

Years later, in 2008, when a *Justice League* DVD I adapted was nominated, we were up against feature-length versions of *Family Guy* and *South Park*, and I immediately assumed that smart, hip, cutting-edge *South Park* would win—but then I spent weeks trying to fashion arguments for a victory of our own: better animation? More elaborate design work? Nope. My first impression was the correct one again.

The way the winners are chosen is substantially different from the nomination process. Panels of volunteer Academy members who aren't connected to any of the nominated shows are asked to vote for their favorites. I've been one of those judges, and I assure you, the selection of the winner is as apolitical as the nominations are political. Thus, the real honor, I believe, is in winning, not in being nominated.

Of course honor isn't necessarily the prime motivation for entering the Emmy derby. One of those awards looks good on a resume, and two look especially good, because the second might be seen as proof that the first wasn't a fluke. When you've got two or more, you are a multi-Emmy winner, and who wouldn't want to hire someone like that? Sounds crass, I know, but it's not called "show *business*" for nothing. And who would you rather work with, someone who coldly appraises the award as something that will help obtain more work in the future, or someone whose only source of self-worth is a gold-colored statuette?

An award like an Emmy can also be a milestone in someone's life. I got my first one when I was in my late forties, which is not usually an age when people start looking back and assessing their lives—they're still too busy looking ahead at what they hope will be prime career time. I would have been doing that too, except for something that happened that night at the Century Plaza.

The previous year, 1997, when we were nominated for *Superman* and I was hoping against hope for a win, coming home empty-handed was a big letdown, even though I'd been pretty sure *Freakazoid* would beat us. So, this next year, I figured — wrongly—we would lose again, but I was intent on enjoying the banquet as best I could. And it was a nice one, with lots of wine being poured continuously by the waitstaff... which made it impossible for me to tell when I passed my normal two-glass limit.

But by the end of the evening, I was pretty sure I had, so, Emmy in hand, I decided to linger at the hotel bar with my wife before taking the wheel of my car. Sipping a Coke, I heard someone call my name. It was a slender, cheerful woman named Chris, who was playing piano at the bar that night. I'd met her years earlier when I was in my mid-thirties and still single, and she was in her early thirties and also single. We were neighbors in Santa Monica, and we had a mutual friend who threw lots of parties at which Chris and I would usually chat briefly and then go off to separate conversations with other people.

There wasn't much of a tale to tell until one day when I ran into her at a bank, and she suggested we set up a lunch. Given what little had transpired between us before this, I was a bit surprised, but nevertheless willing to take a chance. And who knew, if this lunch date went well, maybe there'd be a dinner date somewhere in the future.

But our lunch turned out to be anything but a date. What she wanted to talk about was her boyfriend. She was having some problems with him, and she described the problems in graphic detail. All she needed from me just then was a sounding board, and I wasn't so selfish that I couldn't spare one lunch for that chore.

But it didn't turn out to be just one. A few months later, I ran into her again, and again she suggested lunch. I was still unattached, and maybe it was that that made me wonder if things had gone down the toilet with her boyfriend.

They had, but now she had a new boyfriend, and I had to listen to some very intimate details of that relationship. Never again, I silently vowed. But then more months would pass, I remained unattached, hope still flickered, and since we were still neighbors, we would run into each other periodically. Sometimes she would invite me to a hotel bar where she'd been hired to play piano and sing. I would go, and keep going, until at last, on nothing more than a whim, I broke off one of our "dates" at the very last minute. Ten years would pass before I would run into her again that night at the Century Plaza.

During those ten years, my life had changed a lot: a career, financial stability, a move from my tiny apartment in Santa Monica to a nice house in the suburbs and, most important, I was no longer unattached. And then there was that statuette I'd been handed earlier in the evening. Had my life been fiction, that night would have a good time to finish it, but seeing the piano player again after all those years was almost as good as fiction. No, not because my life had improved so much, while hers looked to be exactly where it had been ten years earlier. And not because I thought for even a moment that she might've had a regret or two about those lunch "dates" not being actual dates. I'll never know for sure, but my best guess is that all that went through her mind when she saw me that night with my wife and my Emmy was, "Oh, there's that guy who used to live near me, he's with someone, and it looks like he won some kind of prize." I doubt if her memory of this latest (and to date, final) chance meeting lasted for even the remainder of the night.

What made the encounter so memorable for me was that it underscored how much my life had changed. I think many people still see themselves as children or teenagers long after they've entered adulthood. The house, the car, the spouse, even children of their own—they can all feel like things that have been merely acquired, rather than earned. In other words, things that happened to you, not things you worked hard for.

That first Emmy certainly felt that way to me, but after a while, and after seeing the piano player again, it finally began to dawn on me that I had really become a different person, not just someone who had obtained the trappings of a different person. Now I was someone who, among other things, would never put up with lunches like the ones I had with the piano player.

And all those things I'd acquired since the last time I'd seen her? They began to feel more like goals I had worked hard to achieve. So, when a second Emmy arrived three years after that night at the Century Plaza, it didn't feel unreal at all. Or surreal.

As we were driving home from the Century Plaza Hotel with that first Emmy in the back seat, my wife asked about the piano player: "Did you date her?"

I took a pause before answering, trying to decide whether or not to tell her the whole story. It might not have sat well, even though it had all taken place years before I met Teagan, who's not known for being without a jealous bone in her body. So, I would have felt perfectly justified telling her I hadn't dated Chris, even if I had. But I didn't need to lie about that, did I?

So all I said when Teagan asked if I'd dated her was, "No," and that was the end of it.

STAN BERKOWITZ

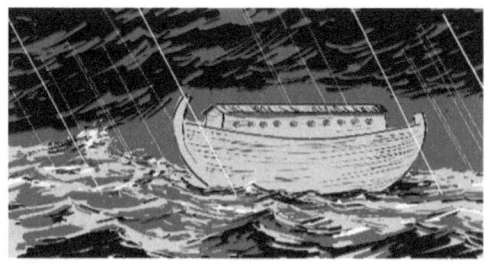

CHAPTER TWO

WRITTEN BY STAN BERKOWITZ... AND GOD: ANIMATING THE BIBLE

They were words every writer should hear at least once in a career: "What do I have to do to make this deal work?" And it didn't hurt that they were coming from the man who produced the first two *Star Wars* movies, Gary Kurtz. Even so, I had some trepidation. If I took the job he was offering, I would have to leave Warner Bros Animation, where I'd been quite comfortable for eight years. There'd be no more medical insurance or pension plan.

And it wasn't as if Gary was offering me a chance to write a *Star Wars* sequel; his working relationship with George Lucas had ended years earlier, and now Gary was producing an animated TV series about the

Bible—a book I was almost totally unfamiliar with. I knew the stories everybody knows, of course: Noah's Ark, Eve and the Apple, Jonah and the Whale, etc., etc., but the book itself just never called to me.

Gary assured me I didn't need to know the Bible, and I didn't even have to be particularly religious to work on the show. And the show did need work, and it needed it soon. Six scripts were already in various stages, but none had been written by experienced animation writers, and it showed. Scenes were too slow or too talky, and a lot of the physical action wasn't described explicitly enough for the artists to adapt to animation.

So, Gary was over a barrel, and the offer he was making was a pretty honest admission of that. To sweeten it, he even agreed to make a deal with the Writers Guild of America to get the show's writers covered by the Guild's pension and health plans, which were actually better than the plans at Warners. That was exactly what I needed to make the deal work, so I took a leap of faith, and the spot where I landed didn't turn out to be quite as unfamiliar as I expected.

Gary's show was called *Friends and Heroes*, and it was conceived by an Oxford professor and Methodist minister named Brian Brown. Brian's academic specialty was the early years of Christianity, before the New Testament was written, when the only means of proselytizing was through storytelling.

Making the task exceedingly dangerous for those ancient storytellers was that the new religion had been born in the Roman Empire, and the Romans weren't exactly sympathetic to it. Thus, *Friends and Heroes*'s fictional protagonists had to spend lots of time dodging the Emperor's bloodthirsty guards, and the only way they could keep their spirits up during their various ordeals was by telling each other inspiring stories from the Old and New Testaments.

So that the tales from the Testaments could be visually differentiated from the framing stories about the early Christian storytellers, the Bible tales were rendered in computer animation, while traditional, flatter-looking 2-D animation was used for the framing stories. Brian would tell us the Biblical stories that he wanted to see in the individual episodes, and we would work out the details of the framing stories to reflect the themes of those Bible stories. Each Bible story would be translated from the original ancient Greek or Hebrew by Brian, and we would then drop the stories into our scripts. Brian wouldn't let us change a word of the Bible stories; not any of the action or even a line of dialogue. On occasion though, we were allowed to choose camera angles for the Bible stories, and when we dramatized the Noah's Ark story, Brian uncharacteristically stepped in to choose some angles himself.

Brian was anything but a literalist, and he'd occasionally offer the writers common sense explanations for some of the Bible's more fantastical moments. The parting of the Red Sea, for example, might have just been a low tide, while Moses's burning bush could have been nothing more than a rising or setting sun "burning" through the foliage. Other tales he'd simply reject, like the one about Jonah, who supposedly survived inside a large aquatic animal for three days, digestive juices be damned.

So, when we were adapting Noah's story, Brian was concerned about the Bible's claim that Noah was 600 years old when he set sail in his ark. Brian simply couldn't imagine what the face of such an old man would look like, so he avoided the issue altogether by telling the writers to show Noah only with his back to camera, which we did. (If you think 600 is old, keep in mind that Noah's dad, Lamech, lived to be 777, and his dad's dad, Methusaleh—yes, *that* Methusaleh—lived to be 969. And unless my math is off, both Lamech and Methusaleh died around the same time, most likely drowning during the Great Flood. Had ungrateful Noah thought to give dad and granddad boarding passes to his ark, the two might still be around today, and probably living in Florida.)

It's easy to laugh off some of this stuff, since a lot of what's described in the Bible makes very little sense to modern readers, but when the voice actors arrived at the recording studio, they needed to be able to find an emotional connection to the material. If that material seemed incomprehensible to them or even slightly ambiguous, it was up to the story editor -- me—to explain. And if I didn't get it, the recording session was guaranteed to be long... and expensive.

To help me, Brian suggested I buy a Bible—not the familiar King James version with its flowery language, its euphemisms and all those "thee's" and "thou's"; instead, he recommended something called the Contemporary English Version or CEV. It's a plainspoken translation, yet it somehow made the contents of the Good Book all the more shocking to me.

Years before this, when I was looking for Biblical quotes to be spouted by a reformed criminal in one of my scripts, I checked a Bible out of the library, but when I started reading it, I had real doubts that this book was the actual Bible. It read more like an elaborate parody. And I couldn't find any good quotes to lift, either.

The CEV convinced me that the book I'd seen years earlier was indeed the real thing; what was wrong were my expectations. I'd always believed the Bible contained the familiar stories, and also was more or less a list of things a good person should and shouldn't do. The CEV had all that, of course, but there was so very much more.

The New Testament, I think, is basically a sales pitch for Christianity. In it, there are accounts of the life of Jesus, each one only slightly different from the other, and there are also the aforementioned rules to live by, articulated by Jesus and supposedly formulated by God himself. The earliest Christians hoped that people would read this new document (or have it read to them, given the low literacy rate during that time) and then become Christians. And it worked phenomenally well. Today, Christianity is the world's number one religion in terms of adherents, edging out Islam by a couple hundred million.

If the New Testament was a sales tool, the Old one was something entirely different. For starters, the Jews weren't, and still aren't, trying to sell their religion to anyone. They do not proselytize, and if they did, gentiles would be well advised to proceed with caution in light of an especially grisly tale from the Old Testament's Genesis chapter. It involves Jacob, son of Isaac, grandson of Abraham and father of many sons, most prominently, Joseph. Jacob also had at least one daughter, Dinah, who must've been an absolute stunner, because after a young gentile named Shechem raped her, he did something rapists don't generally do: he fell head over heels in love with her. So, he went to Jacob to ask for Dinah's hand in marriage.

Dinah's brothers wanted nothing but revenge, so they led Shechem on. They said they'd give him Dinah only if he agreed to be circumcised. And one other thing: all the other men in his tribe would have to be circumcised, too. On reflection, this might sound like an invitation to some kind of weird open marriage, but Shechem was so smitten, he didn't notice. He used his considerable influence with his tribe to get the other men to submit to the procedure, and while they were in a weakened state as they recovered from the surgery, Dinah's brothers killed them all and took their sheep, goats and everything else they had, including their wives and children.

This is a pretty clear warning to gentiles (and genitals!) about conversion, and it's right there at the beginning of the book. When the Christians slapped the Old Testament onto their Testament and published both in the same book, it made a lot of folks forget that the Old Testament was—and still is—a book for, by and about Jews. It wasn't intended as guidance for anyone else. And given the literacy rate back then, it clearly wasn't intended to be read cover-to-cover by most Jews. What it seems to be is a compilation of hundreds of stories that had been part of the Jews' oral tradition for many centuries. Over all those years, various rabbis—whole battalions of them, probably—took on the Herculean task of putting it all on paper for the benefit of future generations of rabbis.

But which versions of the stories would they write down? When you're dealing with an oral tradition in which stories have been handed down for centuries--or even as much as a millennium or two—the stories are bound to be altered during the endless retelling, some to the extent that the same basic story can eventually appear to be two completely different stories. I'll give you an example.

You've probably heard the story of Lot and his unnamed wife, who turned into a pillar of salt, but do you know what happened to Lot after that? It's not talked about much in Sunday school, and you'll soon see why. Lot's story begins with three travelers stopping at the home of Lot's uncle, Abraham. Abraham washes the men's feet and offers them food, and it's a good thing he does, because although these three look like ordinary men, they are not. Two are angels, and one is God himself.

God is so impressed by Abraham's hospitality, he offers Abraham two bits of information. One is that even though Abraham's wife Sarah is thought to be beyond childbearing age, she'll give birth in just a year. That's the good news, though Sarah is dubious. But God's other tidbit is quite disturbing. He tells Abraham he's heard the people of nearby Sodom and Gomorrah are doing a lot of bad things, so he's decided to destroy both towns.

Abraham is terrified by this; his nephew Lot and Lot's wife and two daughters happen to live in Sodom. So, as the two angels head off to Sodom, God sticks around Abraham's place as Abraham bargains with him over the fate of Sodom. Eventually, God agrees that if his two angels can find ten good people in Sodom, he will cancel his radical urban renewal project.

When the two angels get to Sodom, the first person they meet, as luck would have it, is Lot. Lot shows them the same kind of hospitality his uncle Abraham showed them; he takes the men into his home and feeds them, but before they can even get to sleep, the Bible says that "every man" in Sodom came to Lot's door and demanded that the travelers be brought out so they could have sex with them.

So much for ten good people! Or even two. But what about Sodom's women? Where were they in all this? Didn't they count? Perhaps there weren't any living there. The CEV doesn't shed any light on Sodom's distaff side, nor does it say if there even was one. But if there weren't any women in Sodom, where did little Sodomites come from?

As Sodom's men try to break down Lot's door, Lot does something that seems more than a little strange to modern readers: he offers the mob his two virgin daughters in place of the angels.

I'll pause to let that sink in, but the CEV doesn't even take a breath. Apparently, Lot's offer of his daughters is what any good host would have done back in those days. Alas, the mob is not interested in women, and they continue to clamor for the two angels. So, the angels blind them all, then tell Lot to get out of there with his family, and whatever they do, they better not look back.

Lot's wife famously does look back and instantly turns into a block of salt. Lot is so traumatized by all this, he winds up living in a cave with his two daughters. The end? Not quite. As their isolated existence drags on, the daughters start to fear they'll never find husbands. How will they ever have kids? If the Old Testament had been a movie, the two of them would have realized something at the same time, and then slowly turned to look at Lot, sitting in a corner, staring off into space, still traumatized. *Hmmmmm...*

The girls proceed to get Lot so drunk on successive nights, he has no idea what he's doing, and both of them end up pregnant. Did God punish the three of them for this flagrant incest? No, he did not. Instead, Lot becomes the father (and grandfather!) of two boys, one of whom goes on to found the Moabite tribe, and the other, the Ammonites.

Some interpret this story as a condemnation of homosexuality, while others insist that homosexuality is only incidental to the real theme, which is that you must treat strangers with respect and not impose on them in any way. I happen to think it's about something else: the importance of reproducing. These people were a minority then (as now) and they lived in a world where there was no shortage of wars, plagues and other privations (ditto). They needed to be numerous just to survive. And part of survival in those days meant being able to raise a huge army. Hence, there was no punishment for Lot or his daughters; having kids was such a necessity, you had to do whatever you needed to do in order to have them.

The rabbis apparently felt this message was so important, it was worth telling more than once, so another version of the story is slipped into Judges 19 through 21. This one begins with a wife leaving her husband. The Bible, which doesn't name the wife, declares that she was unfaithful, but it's unclear if she got that label because she was having an affair with a Moabite across the road, or simply because she didn't want to be married to this guy anymore. And why wouldn't she want to be married to him? Keep reading.

The husband, whom the Bible calls only "the Levite," simmered for a while after his wife left, then went to his father-in-law's place to see if he could get her back. The father-in-law was happy to oblige and the reunited couple headed back to the Levite's home.

On the way, the couple stops for a night in the territory of the Benjamin tribe—fellow Israelites. An old man they run into invites them to spend the night at his place, but before they can even finish dinner, some of the Benjamin men start pounding on the door. Guess what they want.

Yeah, it's the same thing all over again, and the old man is just as appalled as Lot was that any guest of his should be imposed upon in that way. So, just as

Lot did, the old man offers the mob his virgin daughter, and to sweeten the deal, he tells them he'll throw in the Levite's wife. Unlike the mob in Sodom, this one's predilections are relatively flexible, so they end up taking the Levite's wife for the night.

Why did the Levite allow this to happen? Had he heard Lot's story and figured this is just what you do in these situations? Or was this typical of how men treated their wives and daughters back then? Either way, it's getting easier to see why the Levite's wife left him in the first place, isn't it?

The next morning, the Levite opens the door to find his wife lying on the doorstep. He tells her to get up, it's time to go, but when she doesn't move, he realizes she's dead. Not intentionally murdered by the mob, but literally fucked to death by them. The Levite is outraged; how could fellow Israelites have done such a thing? The gang rape was apparently okay with him, but causing her to die, albeit unintentionally? *That* crossed a line. So, he does what most any new widower would do, I suppose: he cuts his wife's body into twelve pieces and has his servants take the pieces to the leaders of the other tribes of Israel.

If the tribal leaders see anything disturbing about the way this message was expressed, the Bible doesn't mention it. But the leaders are just as appalled as the Levite by the Benjamins's breach of etiquette. This leads not to God destroying the Benjamins's town, but to something almost as destructive: a genocidal internecine war. At the war's end, only a handful of the Benjamin men have survived. Their homes have been burned, and their wives and children slaughtered.

And then came the second thoughts. In the same way Lot's daughters began to think about their progeny once the dust (and ash) settled, the victorious tribes soon began to worry about the future of the Benjamin tribe. But now that all the Benjamin women had been slaughtered, how could the Benjamin men marry and have children?

Before going into battle against the Benjamins, all the other tribes had sworn an oath to never let Benjamin men marry their daughters, so it wasn't as if the Benjamin survivors could now marry into any of the other tribes. Did that mean the end of the Benjamins? Thankfully not. The folks from a place called Jabesh hadn't attended the big meeting when war was declared, and that was a big mistake on their part, because attendance at that meeting wasn't optional; you were cursed if you didn't attend. So the tribal leaders now sent soldiers to accursed Jabesh to kill everyone except the unmarried women.

Unfortunately, this newest slaughter didn't yield enough virgins for all the remaining Benjamins, so something else had to be figured out. At this point, someone came up with a brilliant idea—a little late for the people of Jabesh, but brilliant nonetheless, and unfortunately, the unheralded genius behind the idea is described in the CEV merely has "someone." The gist of the idea was that although the Israelites had sworn not to allow their daughters to marry Benjamins, what if the Benjamins don't ask for permission to marry the girls, and were to simply kidnap them instead?

Were these guys good at finding loopholes, or what?

The Benjamin men were instructed to go to a festival at a place called Shiloh where the unmarried women were scheduled to do a big ritual dance. During the dance, the Benjamin men would swoop in, kidnap them and take them for their wives. Since the girls' fathers weren't going to be tipped off to this ambush, the fathers wouldn't technically be violating their oath to never let their daughters marry Benjamins. The kidnapping went off without a snag, and we are left to assume everyone lived happily ever after. And by 'everyone,' I mean only the men.

Most of the preceding might sound like a tale from another planet, yet I was surprised to see that at least one aspect of it seemed familiar to me. I found myself visualizing the ancient rabbis trying to put all the stories on paper, but arguing endlessly over which version of the stories to use. The Lot and Benjamin stories are clearly distorted versions of a single story, and I can practically see those old rabbis arguing about which one to include in the book, until at last the head rabbi throws up his hands in exasperation and allows both stories to go in, but at different places, in the hope that no one will notice.

It must have been a lot like some of the writers' rooms I sat in at the beginning of my career: a bunch of old men arguing about what should, and shouldn't go into a story. All that would've been missing from the Biblical writers' room would've been cigars and pipes.

The resulting stories, from both the TV writers' rooms and the Bible-era ones, had problems, often with story logic. Why did the characters do some of the things they did? Better not to ask; in the case of the TV scripts, censors' notes or budgetary restrictions or actors' demands might have left viewers with questions that couldn't be answered. In the case of the Bible, the questions have been around for millennium or three, and time and again on *Friends and Heroes*, when I'd ask for an explanation or a clarification of something we were dramatizing, I'd be told that the passage was iconic, couldn't be explained, and just had to be accepted the way it was.

My guess is that the ancient scribes heard pretty much the same thing: that the stories they were putting on paper had been around forever and couldn't be changed. If the characters' motivations seemed illogical or incomprehensible, it was just too bad. Whatever the case, being a writer has helped me understand and even sympathize with those old rabbis.

Needless to say, neither Lot's story, nor the Levite's, nor Dinah's came within a hundred miles of being dramatized on *Friends and Heroes*. It wasn't that kind of show.

Once the early bugs were worked out, writing and production went smoothly, thanks in large part to Brian and a generous investor. And my time with Gary Kurtz turned out to be one of the smoothest working relationships I've ever had. At first, Gary seemed rather cold and impersonal, which surprised me, because his career and his personal life tended toward extremes: combat photography in Vietnam as a conscientious objector, producing the hugely successful *American Graffiti* as well as the first two *Star Wars* movies, then an affair with Carrie Fisher, two divorces, a handful of box office failures and a bankruptcy.

But he never talked about any of that. Neither the good stuff nor the bad. What he always wanted to talk about---with me, anyway---was movies. New ones, old ones. Why they worked or didn't work. He was a convert to Buddhism, but the business seemed to be what really mattered to him---though maybe his Buddhism explains why he always seemed so even-tempered and why he never seemed to get upset or be uncertain---qualities I initially mistook for coldness.

When it came time for the WGA to arbitrate the episodes' writing credits there was a problem or two. Because the scripts for the Bible tales were handed to the writers by Brian, we never needed to write more than 15 or 16 minutes of a 22-minute show, which made the job that much easier for the writers. But some of us wondered who was writing the other six or seven minutes? The Guild has a booklet of rules and regulations designed to make sure everyone involved in the writing of a script is treated fairly in terms of credit, but there was nothing about a situation like this in the booklet.

In regard to the script I wrote, I was happy to take credit for the framing story, but I never even touched the two Bible stories—so who should've gotten credit for that part of the script? Not Brian, since he saw himself as acting only as a translator. What about Matthew, Mark, Luke or John? Maybe, but scholars have doubts about whether some of them even existed.

And had the Guild's credit arbitrators tried to consider the authorship of the Old Testament stories, they would've run into the claim that the book was written by God himself. If they'd accepted that notion, I would have been happy to share a credit with Him, but since I had contributed more pages to the script than He had, I would have wanted first billing. The arbitrators didn't see it that way, so I wound up with sole credit, and God got no credit at all.

STAN BERKOWITZ

I'll probably have some 'splainin' to do when I get to the Pearly Gates.

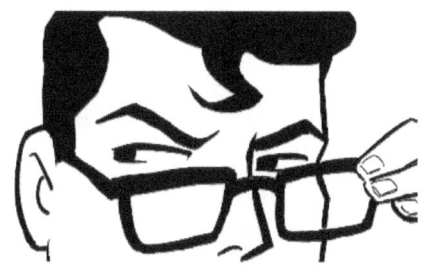

CHAPTER THREE
THE GREEN GROUP

I was on a panel at the 2017 Palm Springs Comic Con, tossing softball interview questions to my old friend Alan Burnett, but he was struggling to answer a question about something I'd been curious about for years. The occasion for our panel was Alan's retirement after more than a quarter-century of writing and producing at Warner Bros Animation, and I wanted to know what had drawn him to the superhero genre in the first place.

Over the twenty-plus years I'd known him, we'd hardly ever talked about anything other than politics, movies and plain old gossip, so my question probably took him by surprise. After I rephrased it, Alan thought for a moment, then did what I'd seen him do in so many story meetings: he came up with a perfect answer.

"I like the secret identity aspect of superhero stories," he said.

Who among us doesn't have a side we keep secret from even our closest intimates? A cynic who's somehow privy to everyone's fantasies might look at our species and see millions of thieves who can't bring themselves to actually steal, philanderers who somehow manage to stay faithful and would-be murderers who'd never kill anyone. As much as we fantasize about doing those things, most of us shy away from the harsh reality and the attendant consequences.

That's not to say our secret fantasies are all anti-social; sometimes we fantasize about heroic things we'd like to do. At its emotional core, the early Clark Kent/Superman dynamic was really about a nondescript person wanting the power to do good things, and, not so incidentally, to impress a girl who won't give him the time of day.

If there actually were a Superman, it would be malpractice on his part to bother with a secret identity, because it would take too much time and effort to maintain. Better to be out saving the world than trying to impress Lois Lane. But for the Superman stories to work, at least in Superman's early years—the secret identity aspect was a necessity, so that young readers could have something to identify with.

Sure, Clark seemed powerless—like a child—but he was actually someone who had well-hidden "powers and abilities far beyond those of mortal men." That's a compelling fantasy for an eight-year-old—and even for some 40-year-olds.

Alan's answer hit a major chord, because the secret identity theme is one of the main reasons superhero stories have endured for so long. But superhero stories have another over-arching theme, and it's the one that attracted me: anti-authoritarianism. Despite paying lip service to the American way and making alliances with the Commissioner Gordons and Inspector Hendersons of their worlds, superheroes constantly make life-and-death decisions on their own, without asking anyone. In essence, they are vigilantes who (mostly) get along with the authorities, but ultimately answer only to themselves.

What happens when a superhero chooses to put loyalty to government ahead of personal principles? See Frank Miller's *Dark Knight Returns* graphic novel for a tale of a fascist Superman versus a Batman who won't knuckle under to an oppressive government. It's brutal.

My own anti-authoritarianism started early. Back in the first grade, my teacher, Mrs. Hamilton, was tasked with figuring out who the fast and slow learners in her new class were. In other circumstances, an IQ test would've been administered, but an IQ test would have required the ability to read, and the reason Mrs. Hamilton needed to differentiate the fast learners from the slow ones was because reading was what she was about to teach us.

There was an easy way to separate us, and that would've been for her to simply ask the kids, because after just a few days on the playground, we all knew who the quick, verbal kids were and who the slower, less verbal ones were. But Mrs. Hamilton had been doing this a long time, and she chose to rely on her instincts -- as well as the prejudices she'd developed over thirty years in the classroom. She sent the little bespectacled kids to the so-called blue table—code for the fast-learners' group—while the big, oafish-looking kids had to sit at the green table, which was for the slow learners.

It so happened that a boy named Gregory and I were the biggest, and possibly most oafish-looking, so we were sent to the green group. Gregory and I were already friends because the class had been lining up by height when we were marched to the cafeteria, so at the first recess after we'd been sent to the green group, he and I had an urgent conversation. If our dialogue from that conversation seems a little too mature to have come from six-year-olds, I'm sorry, but this is how I remember it. What you're about to read is my first adult conversation, and its stakes turned out to be enormous.

"We're in the wrong group. You know that, don't you?" Gregory whispered tensely.

"Yeah," I whispered back, "but what can we do about it?"

Gregory thought for a moment, then offered, "Tell our parents?"

I nodded my agreement.

Our parents quickly got involved, but Mrs. Hamilton wasn't one to be intimidated. She told them that Gregory and I would be moved up to the middle table, the red one, but only if our reading progress warranted it.

It did. Within just days, we were sent to sit with the red group. Then at recess Gregory took me aside again. "We're still at the wrong table," he whispered. We agreed to talk to our parents again, and soon, we were moved to the blue table.

And then came another recess, and Gregory asked me, "What if there was a yellow group?"

I just smiled. Our journey from green group to yellow group didn't take more than a few days.

Families moved around a lot in our neighborhood, and I lost touch with Gregory after first grade. I don't remember his last name, so I don't know if his precocious ambition led him to a captaincy of industry, or if he shone too brightly too early and eventually burned himself out. What I learned from him was how important it would be to always sit at the smart kids' table.

Once the other kids and I knew how to read, written tests were given, and our placement didn't rely so much on our teachers' prejudices. But I've always wondered what would've happened to me if there'd been no Gregory. Would I have acted on my own? Or would I have accepted Mrs. Hamilton's assessment of my potential?

Probably the latter. I'd had a wonderful time the previous year in kindergarten, and school was the only institution I'd ever encountered, so I had total respect for it. If a teacher of mine thought I would have a harder than average time learning how to read, I would have accepted her assessment without question. Would she have eventually seen that I was making faster progress than the other kids in the green group? That would have required her to acknowledge she made a mistake, and Mrs. Hamilton didn't seem to be someone who'd easily make such an admission. As best as I can recall, no one beside Gregory and me was moved from group to group. Did that mean we were the only mistakes she made? Unlikely.

Had I stayed in the green group, would I have done what little was asked of me and then slacked off, thereby justifying Mrs. Hamilton's original assessment? I'm afraid I might have. And what about the other bright kids who were assigned to the wrong table? IQ tests administered in upper grades might've helped them, but I wonder how many of them had by then given in to their teachers' low expectations.

My green group story should be a positive one, a tale that shows how important good friends and caring parents can be. And the icing on the cake would be that there wasn't any lingering resentment on Mrs. Hamilton's part for being corrected like that. She was as helpful as she could have been to Gregory and me for the rest of the year. But the scar has lasted far longer than the Band-Aid, and to this day I remain suspicious of authority figures.

It's not that I've been perpetually skeptical about their all-around competence; my doubts have usually centered on their ability to judge other people's competence. In school, that translated to a less than wholehearted acceptance of my teachers' assessments of my potential, but at work, it became something else entirely: what my bosses thought of me and my work mattered a great deal to me on a practical level, because their opinions would determine if I'd be paid, if I'd get to do more work or if I would be promoted. But if a boss of mine told me every word I wrote was gold—or tripe—it wouldn't affect me emotionally, nor would it change the way I wrote. What did they know?

And what do I know? More than once, I've been in positions similar to Mrs. Hamilton's, trying to guess a stranger's potential. Should this writer or that assistant be hired? Often, there've been writing samples to rely on, but even so, I've been wrong about new writers almost half the time—basically, the frequency of the coin toss.

So, with that in mind, I tend to avoid questions of authority in my scripts, and on those rare occasions when my protagonists do brush up against authority, authority usually loses. On the live-action cop shows I worked on, the cops, who were authority figures themselves, usually didn't act like it. They were just guys who constantly risked their lives to prevent crimes, help innocent people and make sure the guilty faced justice. When their superiors got in the way of them doing the right thing, they would find creative ways to get around them, or they would just take the law into their own hands.

In animation, the superheroes I've written for almost always took the law into their own hands, though it must be said their values usually coincided with those of the civil authorities. I can't recall ever writing a Batman/Commissioner Gordon scene, but I do remember a Superman episode (*The Late Mr. Kent*) when Superman interacted with a tough cop—who turned out to be covering up a murder he'd committed.

In an episode of *Justice League* called "A Better World," I wrote about an alternate world version of the Justice League who took over their world—with only the best intentions, of course. It has a scene in which the American president contacts Superman to see if he would let an election be held that November—"It's kind of a tradition, you know?" the president reminds him—but Superman brusquely says he doesn't think the public is ready for it yet.

That's where contempt for authority leads: you become an authoritarian yourself, and ultimately, more totalitarian than the authority you once defied. At least, that's where it leads in fiction. Real life is a lot messier.

Lately, I find myself wondering what happened to the kids in the green group. In high school, the green group/yellow group concept became more elaborate, with classes labeled everything from HH (high honors) to LL (go ahead, guess). The HH kids and the ones just below were bound for college, but the rest were headed to blue collar jobs or the military, which in those days meant Vietnam. Rarely did I see anyone make a leap like the one Gregory and I made, either upward or downward. Our fates might not have been hermetically sealed in childhood, but the often-arbitrary choices of our teachers would certainly determine how easy or how difficult it would be for some of us to become the people we wanted to be.

One of the things that now troubles me most about the green group situation is that once Gregory and I left their table, we never had a second thought about the kids we left behind. We were so embarrassed by once having been assigned to it, we tried to forget we'd ever been there. In our defense, we might have assumed that those kids would be getting the best education they were capable of absorbing—Mrs. Hamilton would move them along slowly, making sure they would learn everything they needed to learn.

But did either of us think to turn back and help those kids, or maybe even tutor them? Nope. All through elementary school, junior high school and high school I never saw a single instance of students tutoring other students. We were all so busy climbing the ladder, we never took time to look back down.

Now I wonder how the kids who were misjudged by authority figures have turned out. The younger ones seem to find a release in tales of super-powered heroes who live by their own rules and don't have to answer to anyone. But what about the older ones, the ones whose teachers' early assessments ultimately turned some of them into potential cannon fodder? You don't hear from them too much, but they do vote, and when they vote for candidates who promise to rip apart the existing power structure, you can't really be surprised.

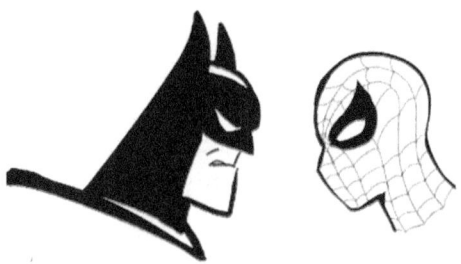

CHAPTER FOUR
WHEN THINGS GO WELL... THERE'S SELDOM A STORY TO TELL

In the late 1980s, a children's TV executive named Jean MacCurdy became head of Warner Bros Animation. The division had an illustrious past, populated by Bugs Bunny, Daffy Duck, Sylvester and Tweetie, Elmer Fudd and others, but it had been relatively inactive for years. Jean and the writers and artists she brought with her changed that. They developed smart, Emmy-winning comedies like *Animaniacs* and *Pinky and the Brain*, and one game-changing superhero show: *Batman: The Animated Series*.

All of these series initially ran on the Fox Kids network, and all of them doubtless had the kind of birthing pains that are associated with friction between network and studio. Both of those entities want shows lots of kids will watch, but getting studio and network to agree on a single creative vision can be a chore. Or worse, a series of battles involving lots of screaming and yelling and firings and hirings.

But what if the same person ran the studio *and* the network? That's what I was looking at in early 1996 when I was hired to be a story editor on Warners Animation's new *Superman* series. The giant Time Warner conglomerate had just started their own network, the WB, and none other than Jean MacCurdy was selected to head its kids' division. She was also continuing to run Warners Animation.

What that meant for those of us who worked for her was that friction between studio and network couldn't exist. There'd be no fighting between network and studio reps for control of the shows—no conflicting sets of script notes, nothing. And even better, at least for me, was the fact that Jean liked writers.

At a traditional animation studio, the lead animators are usually considered the auteurs, but Jean clearly favored the writers. She'd meet with her two dozen or so writers one morning a week, but there'd be no similar meeting with the artists. We'd all get together in a conference room where there was a big marble table shaped like the Warner Bros logo. The stated purpose was for each of us to give her a progress report on whatever we were writing, but it was really more like semi-improvised entertainment for her. A few of us had actually been standup comedians, so the meetings were often just plain comedy—two dozen court jesters performing for a benevolent monarch who needed a weekly laugh or two.

With studio and network working in lockstep, and being run by someone who trusted her creative teams, the only notes the writers usually got were from the writer-producers who ran the different shows. In my case, that writer-producer was Alan Burnett, who was seemingly egoless and unfailingly constructive. So, things went well on *Superman*. We had job security, and we would hardly ever miss an Emmy awards banquet.

Jean might have been a monarch, but she didn't have absolute power. There were people in the conglomerate she had to answer to, and though these people usually didn't give script notes, they did read numbers. The most important set of numbers consisted of ratings, and when the *Superman* show debuted to lower than hoped-for numbers, the show's staff got a clear reminder that Jean wasn't all-powerful. Instead of the promised sixty-five episodes, the WB network executives cut the *Superman* order back to just fifty.

STAN BERKOWITZ

The good news was that the crew would continue working, but now they'd be making brand-new episodes of the animated *Batman* series. This shift was an indication of things to come, but whatever ominousness there was couldn't hold a candle to the good news that we would be getting to work on a continuation of the highly regarded *Batman* show with its dark undertones and hero who would be much easier to write for than the big blue Boy Scout whose nearly limitless superpowers made it difficult for us to put him in dire jeopardy.

The *Batman* reboot went smoothly, and when that ended, most of the crew moved on to the *Batman Beyond* show. But ratings never leapt skyward. The reason, I think, was that cable was coming into its own back then, and the viewership pie kept being sliced thinner and thinner because there were so many more shows to choose from. But try telling that to the companies that make toys, cereal and candy, whose advertising money helps pay for the existence of the network. These companies need kids to watch the shows they sponsor, and when not enough of them do, it's time for a change.

So, four years after I got to Warners Animation, Jean was replaced as head of the Kids WB—but she remained in charge of Warners Animation. Things should have continued to run smoothly, because the same conglomerate still owned both entities, but that wasn't the case, because two different *people* now ran those entities. My theory is that no one gets into the entertainment business by being meek or passive; it's a business that doesn't want or need you, and to get in, you need to be… well, if not ruthless, then certainly competitive by nature. And if that *is* your nature, you can't just shut it off; you've got to dominate, always. Even when everyone's playing on the same team.

Notes started coming to us from the new people at the network, and in no small quantity. A turning point for me came while I was working on a show called *Static Shock*. The new boss of the Kids WB had a background in marketing, and in conducting focus groups with children to see how to improve ratings, she discovered that the kids didn't like villains. They're not supposed to, the writers responded. But that response just showed her how imperfect our understanding of kids was. To make *Static*'s stories more friendly to them, we would now have to leave out villains.

It was a ridiculous order, of course, but also the kind of challenge I found irresistible. Since the show's young superhero had acquired his powers because of an electrical mutation, I wondered what would happen if a solar storm—sunspots—made his powers go haywire. They'd be all but gone one minute, then over-the-top the next. The concept seemed to work, and I was even allowed to have a villain in it… but only as a minor character.

Near the beginning of the episode, I had Static try to leap over a building, but because of the sunspot effect, his power was super-charged at that moment—unbeknownst to him—and he ended up zooming far off into a desert, crash-landing amid cacti and coyotes.

I needed a line of dialogue for him to say as he sat there in the sand, dumbfounded by what had just happened. A real person might've exclaimed, "Jesus!" or "Holy shit!" but the censor obviously wouldn't have tolerated either response. A simple "Whoa!" might have worked, but even back then, that line had been used far too much. So I tried, "I better get frequent flyer miles for this!" You might wonder what a child would know about frequent flyer miles, and frankly, so did I, but I couldn't think of a better line. Still can't.

Soon enough, the network notes came in, and they did want me to change that line, but not because it might be over the kids' heads or because it wasn't very funny. They asked if I could please change the line to, "I *hope* I get frequent flyer miles for this." It took me a while to figure out the difference, but I finally realized that saying, "I better get" something is aggressive speech, while to *hope* for something isn't. I made the change, then went straight across the hall to accept an offer that had been made earlier that day to write for *Justice League*, a new Warners Animation show that would run on Cartoon Network, not the Kids WB.

How different were the Cartoon Network notes from the Kids WB notes? All you need to know about that comes in the form of a single example. One of *Justice League*'s early episodes was an Aquaman story in which the hero's hand gets stuck in a trap, and to save himself, he has to chop it off. The Cartoon Network censor called to ask if the amputation would be shown on screen or if we planned to cut away from it. The producer told him we planned to cut away.

"Good," the censor said. "That's my only note."

I can't remember any other notes we might've gotten from him… or if there were any at all.

The other set of numbers that Jean's bosses kept an eye on were budgets, and after a few more years, Jean's position as head of Warners Animation was taken by an executive whose expertise was cost-cutting. Jean was only in her early 50s at this point, but she was able to transition into a comfortable retirement in San Francisco. Back in Sherman Oaks, Warners Animation went on as usual, albeit with more notes, less job security, fewer Emmy banquets and no weekly writers' meetings with the new boss. So, just a few years after Jean retired, when I got an appealing offer from a European company, I took it.

Was my time at Warners a golden age? Or did it merely seem that way because of what I had gone through just before I got to Warners? Be warned, the answer has nothing to do with things going well.

Two years before starting at Warners, I was at loose ends, so when a writer I'd met on the live-action *Superboy* show told me about a new animated superhero series that was starting at Marvel Animation, I decided to take a chance. I hadn't done animation before, but since I'd just spent a year in the superhero world with *Superboy*, I figured I might be up to the challenge. There'd be less dialogue than in live action scripts, shorter scenes and the action sequences would have to be described in more detail than in live action. Other than that, the transition to animation writing would be easy.

I sent the head writer a *Superboy* script I'd written and heard back pretty quickly: I would be coming aboard in just a few days. That was in October of 1993. Weeks went by, and when I tried to contact the head writer again, I was told by a secretary that he was gone. "Who replaced him?" I asked, without even taking a moment to reflect on his firing. Sounds cold, but I'd never actually met the poor guy, didn't know the circumstances of the firing, and above all, I wanted to start working again. I was about to be married, and I was pretty sure that two had no chance of living as cheaply as one. The secretary gave me the name of the new head writer, I re-sent my sample and was hired again. It was now February, and I was about to become one of a half dozen staff writers helping to script sixty-five episodes of *Spider-Man: the Animated Series* for Fox Kids.

The new head writer was John Semper, a Harvard grad and dedicated comic book fan for whom this was the job of a lifetime. Unflappable, and with a gift for diplomacy, John was an easy man to work for, but I soon found myself wondering who John worked for. And I'll bet John often wondered the same thing.

That was because there were four entities battling for control of the show: Fox Kids, the Marvel Animation studio, Marvel Comics, and Toy Biz, the company that was making the toys that would be sold alongside the series. Representatives of each of these entities believed they should have the final word on scripts—which would've been fine for the writers if they agreed on everything. But they seldom did, and at the beginning of my two years there, there seemed to be no set hierarchy among them.

No one knew who was ultimately in charge—which went a long way toward explaining why the show's half-hour pilot script was taking months to write. And it shouldn't have. Stan Lee's *Spider-Man* storylines and dialogue were far more animation-friendly than the DC Comics world. His characters always had distinct voices and motivations, as opposed to the Silver Age DC comic book characters, whose word bubbles often seemed interchangeable.

(After *Spider-Man*, when I was writing for the *Justice League* series at Warners, I had to ask my boss how Hawkgirl's personality differed from Wonder Woman's, if it did at all. "Let me put it this way," my boss said, "Hawkgirl is married, and Wonder Woman isn't.")

Despite what I considered a crystal-clear guidepost in the form of the old *Spider-Man* comics, no one could seem to agree on how to translate the stories into a pilot. If a draft we wrote pleased one of the four entities, one, two or all three of the others would reject it... which seemed especially odd because the rep for Marvel comics was Stan Lee himself.

Stan was in his early seventies at the time, still very active, very sharp and rumored to be making $1 million a year... which, in those days, would have allowed him—on a yearly basis—to buy four houses like the one I'd been saving so long for. Stan mostly wanted the animated versions of his characters to sound as close as possible to the comic book versions... which particularly irked the network rep, who would constantly complain that Stan's dialogue reeked of the 1940s and needed to be modernized. As a mere staff writer, I would make the dialogue changes the network requested, a new draft would be sent out, and then Stan would see the network's changes and ask that his dialogue be reinstated. So we would make his changes, and when the next draft came out, the network rep would ask that the previous dialogue be reinstated.

I was writing in circles, and even though I shouldn't have minded because I was being paid by the week, it eventually became too much. I took Stan aside and told him that I was basically stealing from the company, getting paid to go in circles. Stan was an icon in the comics world, of course, but the first Spider-Man and Avengers movies were still years away at this point, so he was not yet the international celebrity he would eventually become. To me, he was just an older, experienced writer from whom I expected some fatherly advice.

But all he said was, "Don't worry about it."

So, I didn't, and continued making everyone's changes.

Somehow—and after many more drafts—everyone signed off on the pilot script. Broadcast deadlines probably had a lot to do with it, but whatever the reason, we were soon able to begin work on a three-episode story that would feature the Venom character. To no one's surprise, it didn't go smoothly, either.

We wrote outline after outline, and all of them were rejected by one party or another. Finally, I suggested to John that we host a big meeting where all four parties would be in the same room at the same time, so they could work out the story together. It would be a story meeting, but one in which three of the four main participants weren't writers. It wasn't just frustration that motivated me to suggest this, it was also something approaching sadism — because I knew it would be painful, but I was pretty sure that once it happened, we would never have to go through it again.

The meeting began in the morning, with everyone trying to figure out what the first scene would be. John, whom I'd seen lay out whole stories quickly and efficiently, was not called upon to do what he could have done so easily. Instead, he found himself in the role of moderator. And I was little more than a recording secretary. With the exception of Stan, these were guys who weren't writers, and looking back, I get the feeling Stan wanted to make sure they would realize that by the end of the meeting. So did the other Stan.

The man from Toy Biz was Avi Arad, an Israeli immigrant who would made a fortune with his toys and later go on to executive produce many of Marvel's live action superhero movies. Like many non-writers, he seemed to view storytelling as a matter of stringing together lots of cool action scenes, as opposed to making a single unified statement. He also wanted to cram in as many characters from the Spider-verse as he could, because it would help promote the action figures he was trying to sell.

He was barely skirting broadcast rules, which at that time didn't allow kids' TV shows to be naked advertisements for toys and similar products. So the network rep couldn't have been happy about Avi's intentions, but then again, as a dyed-in-the-wool contrarian, the rep wasn't happy about much that he saw or heard.

His contrarianism had served him well at the beginning of his career in kids' TV, when most of the stuff was condescending crap, and he needed writers and artists to think differently and try new things. At story meetings, though, contrarianism just made the meetings last longer. He'd sit quietly, waiting for everyone else to make their suggestions, and only then would he speak up, and, with impeccable logic, explain why none of it would work.

The fourth party in our story meeting was a gifted artist who was the head animation producer. He viewed *Spider-Man* as a series that, like the comic, would be set in the real world, and in keeping with that sensibility, he doggedly opposed one of Avi's ideas: having a space shuttle land on New York's George Washington Bridge. Why? Aside from the obvious impossibility of such of feat, the bridge also happened to be perpendicular to what would have been the route of the shuttle's orbit, and space shuttles didn't have the kind of maneuverability that would have allowed them to make a ninety-degree turn in midflight.

Wisely, the writers didn't get involved in this particular argument, and Avi eventually got his way, because who would know or care that the orbit and the bridge weren't parallel? Just one person in the whole world, it seemed. Avi also got his way when he insisted that a character called Rhino needed to make a cameo appearance on the bridge right after the shuttle crash-landed—only to be almost immediately run off by the hero without accomplishing much of anything... except for being a reminder that a plastic version of him was available at toy stores everywhere.

When Avi started describing the next cool scene he wanted, Stan finally had enough. He stood up and told Avi that what he was doing was proposing "a series of incidents, not a story."

I'll always respect Stan for saying that. It's no secret that very young children mostly pay attention to action sequences, rather than the scenes that lead up to them. But these preliminary scenes explore character and, if done properly, they'll set in motion the conflict that inevitably leads to the physical confrontation. Without them, all you'd have would be a bunch of fighting that would lack any context.

Would kids watch that? Probably. But should they be pandered to that way? Old school writers like Stan didn't think so. For them, writing properly structured stories, even for children, was akin to giving them a balanced diet, as opposed to an endless feast of ice cream and cupcakes. But feasts—whether of sugar and starch or of fights and explosions—do attract kids, and over the succeeding years, the "balanced diet" argument eventually lost.

If there's any doubt about that, compare an animated *Batman* episode from the early 1990s to an *Avengers Assemble* episode from around 2015. The *Batman* episode would seem quite slow in comparison to the *Avengers* episode, which would feel like a cornucopia of fights and explosions, with the fate of the planet hanging in the balance… and all within just the first seven minutes.

In the long run, sensibilities like Stan's were left in the dust, and his advice didn't have much effect at our big story meeting, either. What did have an effect was the ponderous length of the meeting, and how little was accomplished. "This story stuff is hard," Avi finally remarked over a late lunch of pizza and Snapple. Again, the writers in the room said nothing.

Perhaps it was fear of having to sit through another of these meetings, or maybe everyone felt they'd been heard, but whatever the reason, the notes became slightly less onerous after this very long day. As the season progressed, the writing staff eventually found a rhythm. John would verbally bang out an episode's outline in an hour or two, I would stay home and write an occasional script or do a rewrite, and then once a week, I would read that week's script over the phone to the network rep and jot down his notes. Then we'd address Avi's script notes, which would occasionally come to us on audio cassettes.

You might be wondering who won the big power struggle. Certainly not the writers; the early firing of the first head writer showed just how expendable we were. And it wasn't the animation producer either, because he too was an expendable hireling. Surprisingly, so was Stan Lee. Despite his golden reputation and his big salary, Stan was still just a writer.

That left the network and Avi slug it out. But why would there have to be a power struggle in the first place? Didn't the network and Avi want the same thing – a hit show (which they eventually got)? Of course they did, but once again, there was that need for dominance at all costs. Money played a big part too, and at the end of the day, everyone except Avi was a salaried employee.

But there was no victory party, no single moment of triumph, just a gradual realization on everyone's part that Avi would be the 800-pound gorilla. As an entrepreneur who'd invested a fortune in the *Spider-Man* toys, Avi had the most to lose. So he had to have the last word, and by sheer force of personality and indefatigability, that's what he got.

Had he not bulled his way through like that, the show might still be in pre-production after all these years, and I wouldn't have had quite the appreciation I would soon have for a certain benevolent monarchy.

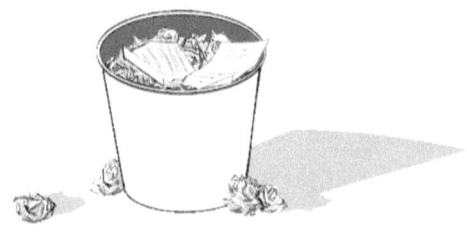

CHAPTER FIVE
NOTES ON NOTES

Reading the preceding chapter, you might have gotten the impression that notes are an unmitigated evil, an ego-motivated power play, a hindrance to production, and, above all, a destructive intrusion into the creative process.

THE END

But seriously, I once attended a writers' award dinner where part of the entertainment was video footage of screenwriters talking about the stupidest notes executives had ever given them. (I was one of those screenwriters, but I insisted that all the notes I'd ever gotten showed unmatched insight and remarkable wisdom, and I was hoping to receive lots more in the years to come. The audience sensed a certain amount of sarcasm.) At conventions, I've seen entire panels devoted to writers telling tales of clueless executives and their idiotic notes. And needless to say, bad notes are a common topic of conversation anytime there's more than one writer in a room.

Can we be the same people who eagerly thrust our spec scripts at you and then badger you with emails, demanding to know what you thought of them—in other words, asking for—no, *begging* for notes?

Yep, we're the same people, but we're hoping for one specific note and no other. And that is, "Your spec script is wonderful, I wouldn't change a word of it, and tomorrow morning, I'll give it to a producer I know." If you say anything other than that, you might as well be talking to a deaf person.

Among the notes writers hate most are those that originate in focus groups — supposed scientific polls of select groups of viewers, where the end product can be as asinine as the note that the writers got when a focus group of children said they didn't like a show's villains. Then there are notes based on purely commercial considerations, like a request to write in a couple of devices that could later be turned into toys—such as a spaceship and underwater breathing apparatus for a little plastic Superman, a representation of a character who would never, ever need either of those gadgets.

Maybe an executive will make a more general complaint, like a story is too dark or not dark enough. Or they'll want to see more of something or less of something else. Non-writers almost always see scripts as collections of moments rather than as organic narratives. A non-writer will seldom say something like, "If you change this one thing here, this other story element somewhere else will work better." They don't think like that. If a script's not working for a non-writer, they'll usually ask for elements to be added or deleted. Less talk! More explosions!

It's even worse when execs just shrug and say a story needs to go in a different direction—without specifying what that direction should be. That's the worst kind of criticism; vague, unconstructive and bad for the show.

A lot of this nonsense comes from a feeling on the part of executives that script notes are a necessity. But are they? Next to the leading cast members, the writers are usually the highest-paid people on the show, and all that money is presumably paying for a level of expertise that shouldn't need much guidance.

But that logic doesn't have as much weight as you might think.

Years ago, on the *Superboy* show, a young Viacom representative was one of the note givers. Reasonable enough, in that Viacom was financing the show. But this kid was more interested in becoming a musician, so I hardly ever got notes from him. When he finally left the show to pursue his muse full-time, our supervising producer was worried; who would now give Stan his Viacom notes?

"Nobody?" I suggested.

My suggestion was ignored and a production assistant in her mid-twenties soon became the new Viacom rep… only days after being the person whose job was to sweep litter from the set.

Somebody who was earning about one-twentieth of my salary would in effect be telling me how to write scripts? If that was such a good idea, couldn't the company have saved a lot of money by putting her in charge of the script department and getting rid of me? That didn't occur to me until later, and thankfully it apparently never occurred to my bosses.

My immediate concern was getting this newbie onto my side, or at least getting her to understand how the script process worked, so that she wouldn't muck it up with ill-timed or impossible-to-address notes. So, I set up a get-acquainted dinner with her, and guess what? I never got a single note from her. Was she intimidated? Or did she think the scripts were okay as written? Or, after that one dinner, did she just not want to have any more contact with me? It could have been all three, but I wasn't about to rock the boat by asking; I was already getting enough notes from other sources: actors, directors, DC comics, line producers, censors—seemingly anyone who could hold a red pencil.

If writers can take any small amount of solace from all this, it's that entertainment industry executives tend to have shorter careers than writers, and once they're done, they're not prepared to do much else in life because their so-called skills are so specific. So, today's ruthless script butchers often end up as tomorrow's real estate agents or among the long-term unemployed, or—and this is true—in the massage business. (The joke that went around about this ex-executive was that he'd always complained that the stories he was overseeing were too dark, and now he'd found himself in a career where happy endings were highly regarded.)

There are other kinds of notes, of course, and they're not all useless. Among the helpful ones are those that involve story logic, which sometimes gets trampled in the rush to tell an emotionally compelling tale. I'll give you an example: I was just working on a script for a graphic novel whose story involved the theft of some medicine that was desperately needed to combat an epidemic. See if you can spot the problem that we didn't notice until the next-to-last draft, after my colleagues and I had gone over and over it.

The story begins with a gang of thugs hijacking a truck the medicine is in; the hero goes to work tracking down the desperately needed drug, all the while suspecting that the gang had been tipped off to the shipment by someone in the government.

Soon, the drug begins to show up on the street. The gang is marketing the stuff the same way they sell recreational drugs, and, just as they did with those illicit drugs, they've diluted the medicine so they can sell more of it. When the people who take the medicine end up in the emergency room, the hero makes an alarming discovery: the liquid the gang used to dilute the medicine caused a chemical reaction the gang could not have anticipated: it turned the drug into poison.

In his effort to track down and destroy the tainted medicine, the hero discovers the identity of the official who tipped off the gang, but this official didn't realize that his new underworld partners would dilute the medicine. When the hero finally confronts this corrupt official, he sees that the man has already given a dose of the tainted medicine to his ailing son, and the boy has just died. Karmic justice!

Except something was missing from that next-to-last draft. As it stood, the corrupt official didn't yet know that his partners diluted the medicine, nor did he know that their amateur chemistry accidentally created a powerful poison. So, when his little boy dies, for all the official knows, the medicine just didn't work. Of course, the readers know that the man has just suffered a particularly brutal form of karmic punishment for partnering with the thugs, but as that draft stood, the official wasn't aware of any of that.

After many long notes sessions, my colleagues and I finally realized what was missing from that final scene: the hero needed to tell the official how he had been betrayed by his criminal partners, and only then should the son die… with the official now knowing exactly how the unintended consequences of his corrupt machinations caused his son's death.

Another example: I have a friend who writes mystery novels, and, like most mysteries, they're "closed": narratives where neither the hero nor the readers know who the killer is until the end. Inevitably in such stories, the killer doesn't stop at the first murder. He continues to kill, bumping off witnesses and making attempts on the life of the hero. Thus, my friend's challenge is to make the story compelling and, of course, logical, but at the same time he must handle a secondary, largely unseen story: the killer's narrative.

In these kinds of stories, you seldom see what the killer is doing while he's doing it, but you always see the effects (i.e.: the dead witnesses). The killer has his own complex narrative, which starts with motive, goes through those successful and unsuccessful attempts on the lives of the witnesses and the hero, and ends with a dramatic reveal, where the secondary, or under-story, finally comes to light.

Though it makes good reading to have a body fall out of a closet every now and then, the writers who invent these moments can't ignore the narrative going on beneath the main narrative. This sub-narrative requires rigorous logic. Was the killer always in the right place at the right time to be able to kill his victims? Did the killer show up in the surface story at a time and place which would've made it impossible for him to commit one or more of these murders? Did he know where to find his victims? If so, how did he know? Is the killer in two places at once? Does he know more than he could possibly know? Does he seem to know less than he should? Does he act (or not act) on this knowledge in a timely fashion? These questions and lots of others need to be answered. Otherwise, there'll be an embarrassing moment at a book signing when someone asks a question about the plot the author can't answer.

So, the editor—or the author's friend—goes through the book's entire outline, keeping in mind this second, underlying narrative, making sure it is consistent with the surface narrative. And, like that surface narrative, it has to conform to the rules of time, space and logic, and its character motivations need to make emotional sense.

It's a lot of work for the author, whose main concern is the surface story, and who might miss a tiny detail in the underlying narrative that could blow up the entire plot. That's when friends and editors help out with notes.

On a writing staff for a TV series, notes are inescapable, and it's nice when they come from a friend. In 1987, I was in a writers' room for a cop show called *Houston Knights*. Presiding was the showrunner, Greg Dinallo, whose staff spent most of the day in his large, accommodating office, talking about story ideas and giving notes on the scripts that came in.

One such script was from a freelancer, and it read like it had been written in less time than it took to read. It was bland and riddled with clichés, and as we sat in Greg's office, the writers offered our unanimous verdict: this script was awful. Greg agreed, but then he did something he hadn't done before: he told us his door would be closed to us when he sat down with this freelancer to give him notes for his second draft.

What could Greg say to this guy? I wondered. The script seemed like a total loss, written by someone who showed no promise of turning in anything better. Yet when the second draft arrived a week later, it was better. Still in need of work, but reading as if it had been written by different writer.

I wanted to know what Greg had said to the writer. Greg told me that he had known this writer for a while and was pretty certain something was going on outside his professional life that was affecting his work. So, after they'd spoken for only a few minutes, the man told Greg that his wife had left him during the week he wrote that first draft.

That writer was lucky to have a sympathetic showrunner in his corner. I once heard an approach similar to Greg's being used by another showrunner, and the result wasn't nearly as pleasant. In this other case, the man behind the desk was the esteemed writer/producer, Roy Huggins. Huggins had started as a noir novelist and then written features and created classic TV series like *77 Sunset Strip*, *The Fugitive* and many, many others. By the mid-1980s, Huggins was in his early seventies, and an executive producer of a cop show called *Hunter*. Unlike Greg DiNallo, Huggins didn't care about discretion when he met with writers; he insisted on taping his notes sessions, and during a long drive from Santa Monica to Burbank, I was able to listen to one of those tapes.

The tape started benignly enough, much as that other freelancer's meeting with Greg must've started. Huggins was inquiring about this young freelancer's health: had he been feeling all right lately? Was anything wrong? The young writer said he was feeling fine, and that's when Huggins sprung his trap. If this young writer hadn't been ill, what other excuse could there be for a particular line of dialogue Huggins was looking at just then? Not only did it not work for this script, Huggins declared, no human being who'd ever lived would have spoken a line like that. Huggins went on that way for another 45 minutes.

This wasn't an isolated incident; another young writer who had been through a similar meeting with Huggins told me that as Huggins went over his draft, he'd rip out every page that had something on it that annoyed him... and he ripped out plenty. The writer broke into tears, and at the end of the meeting he meekly asked Huggins if he could have those torn-out pages back, so he could learn from what he'd done wrong. Huggins, he said, seemed pleased by that.

Why was Huggins doing this? Was he trying to toughen up these young writers to prepare them for a brutally competitive industry? It didn't sound that way; these were writers he wouldn't be doing any more business with, so why was he bothering to even talk to them? Didn't he have more important things to do? From his tone on the tape, it sounded to me like he was just plain fed up, out of patience, and angry that, sometime in the not-so-distant future, kids like these would be sitting behind his desk.

Huggins's story, and also Greg Dinallo's, are both outliers. What usually happens when a seriously substandard script comes in is that the writer is not asked to rewrite it. Because of production deadlines, the staff doesn't have time to wait around for what they fear would be another substandard draft from the writer. It would also be a waste of the writer's time, not that the staff would care much about that. The writer would be thanked for his first draft, told, "the staff will take it from here," and then be paid. Then the staff would go to work on a second draft.

Being neither as empathetic as Greg Dinallo nor as bitter as Roy Huggins, this was my usual approach. An episode of the *Superboy* show that I recall all too vividly even after 30 years involved a writer who turned in a near-perfect draft of a story outline. It had a good comic book-style premise with the potential for plenty of character stuff for the lead actors, and there was a cleverly conceived twist ending, too. I looked forward to the script he would base on this outline, but when it came in via fax late on a Friday afternoon, I quickly saw that it exploited none of the potential I'd seen in the outline.

The dialogue was bland and generic, and the action descriptions were desultory at best. What the writer had done was take the outline I'd approved and simply added some dialogue to it. And it read as if he'd spent no more than a day doing it, with enough time left over for a long lunch and maybe a nap afterwards.

I had taken the script home with me that Friday afternoon, planning to go over it while having a steak at the local Bennigan's. Halfway through my meal, a waitress came over, wanting to know if I was all right. I looked ill.

What notes could I have given this writer? Make the next draft less… empty? Less colorless? Have the characters talk like people? I couldn't think of anything to say to him that would have led to any kind of improvement.

So, as I had done before and would do again over the years, I thanked this writer, authorized payment for him, and then, on Monday morning, I slapped the script down on my staff writer's desk, told him what I thought was wrong with it and gave him a blank check to see what he could do with it. I couldn't have been any more specific than that.

After reading the staffer's first rewrite, I asked him to do a second one, and to make it more personal this time. In his next draft, that's exactly what he did. Then I did a polish of that draft, and when the director arrived, he gave us some notes about the ending which we quickly incorporated. And just like that, the completed episode turned out to be one of our best, an episode that fulfilled all the expectations the outline generated, and which ultimately displayed just that first writer's name as the writing credit.

The supervising producer, who was unaware of all the rewriting that had gone into this episode, saw the writer's name on screen and urged me to give him another assignment.

"Too busy," I said. What I meant was, *I* was too busy.

The best use of the note-giving process, I've found, is when it's guided by the person receiving the notes. When I was in my thirties and still not making a living as a writer, I wrote a spec script that I was pretty happy with, but I wanted to make sure that anyone who read it would understand everything. So, after my then-agent read it, she and I went over it page by page, so I could ask if everything I was trying to say was coming across clearly.

In all the years since, I have never encountered a reader, editor or note-giver as perceptive, sensitive and thorough as she was. All her notes were constructive, carefully considered and ultimately, very valuable. So why is she my "then-agent"?

After finishing that script, and while she was shopping it around to her contacts, I quickly wrote another spec feature. This one, I felt, might have been a good vehicle for Clint Eastwood, so I asked her to send it to his company. It came back unread, and when I asked why, she told me it was because agents needed to work out of a physical office, otherwise they weren't considered accredited, and this agent worked out of her apartment. So, Eastwood's company returned my script unread. There are too many legal risks for production companies to deal with unrepresented writers, and to Eastwood's company, that's what I was: unrepresented.

With no other options for representation at that point, I continued on with that agent, figuring not every producer, especially not the independent ones, would be so finicky about who was representing me, and I was right. An independent producer to whom my agent had sent that first script set up a lunch where I met him and an actor who he thought should play the lead in that script.

Nothing came of it, but after just a few days I got another call from this producer, and he wanted to know if I would do him a favor. He was looking for an agency for himself, and had approached a small but powerful one that represented lots of producers, directors and writers.

I'd first heard of this agency a year earlier, while spending a few days in a TV production office researching an article I was writing for *Esquire*, and I got the impression that the agency represented all the writers in the office. Now this agency wanted to see samples of the kind of script my new producer friend intended to produce, so he was asking if he could show them mine. Why not, I said.

A few days later, someone from that agency called to see if I was happy with my current representation. "Not happy enough," I said.

Thanks to my new agency, six months later I was finally starting to make a living as a full-time writer. I stayed with that small but powerful agency for eighteen life-changing years, but even with all their influence, they couldn't sell those two spec screenplays, either. They did keep me very busy though, and that first spec script, the one my previous agent went over so carefully, got me lots of work and eventually turned out to have an entirely unexpected value: when I first started seeing Teagan, she told me she wanted to write scripts, so I gave her that one as a sample. Much later, she told me that reading it made her fall in love with me… which is a pretty nice note for a writer to get, even if it couldn't be entirely true.

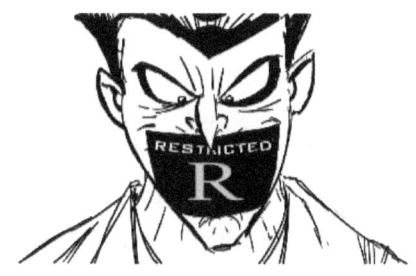

CHAPTER SIX
SUPERHEROES GROW UP...
BUT SHOULD THEY?

If you're ever summoned to the set while you're in a big production meeting, it won't be because the crew wants to throw you a surprise party. When it happened to me once while I was producing the *Superboy* TV series, I was sure it wasn't going to be anything good, but there was no way I could have imagined what I was about to see when I opened the soundstage door. It was our Lana Lang, Stacy Haiduk, and she was holding a large green flaccid phallus.

"I'm not putting this thing on my head," she said to me, by way of a greeting.

Here's another tip: before you say anything, it's sometimes wise to wait a moment. Or even two, because every now and then, someone might step in to offer you a helping hand. This time it was the director, Hugh Martin. Before I could even ask Stacy what was going on, Hugh hurried over to me with a small button-like thing he thought would make a good substitute for the phallus. It could be pasted to Stacy's neck, he said, and with just a line or two of expository dialogue, we could make it clear to the audience that our alien villain was using extraterrestrial technology to download a copy of the contents of Lana's brain, just as the original prop would have supposedly done, had it not looked so very, very much like a phallus.

I instantly approved Hugh's suggestion and hurried back to the production meeting before anything else could be dumped in my lap. But I couldn't stop wondering how something like this could have happened. I'd designed the brain-copying apparatus myself, and in my mind's eye, it looked nothing like a phallus.

Nor did the drawing I made for our prop man. I'd sketched a flat, triangular flap of membrane that would have fit over the front of Stacy's scalp. It would have looked a bit like a prominent widow's peak—except it was going to have a bunch of tiny sucker pads growing out of its edges. So I was more than a little curious to know how this device could have turned into a big green dildo.

After our production meeting, I took the line producer aside and told him what happened. He said he'd seen the prop man's first version of the prop a few days earlier and had told him it looked like "a penis with legs." So had the prop man gone away from that encounter thinking, "penis *with* legs: bad. Therefore, penis *without* legs: good!"? Who knows?

If you're trying to understand how this prop man could have brought a big green phallus to the set that day without having it occur to him that the thing might create a problem or two, and also, why he wasn't instantly fired, there's a single fact that might answer both of those questions: the prop man was also the crew's marijuana supplier, and being his own best customer, he probably thought the sight of a woman with a dildo on her head would be absolutely hilarious. And what would be the big deal anyway, it was just some stupid kids' show, wasn't it?

From their origin in the late 1930s, all the way to the early '60s, superhero comics and their accompanying TV shows and movies were strictly for children, and in the minds of many (including, I suspect, our prop man), that meant they were also childish. Filmmakers, by and large, were happy to feed this stereotype. Check out the animated *Super Friends* or the live-action Batman and Superman serials from the 1940s. Cheap-looking and stupid, most of them. Even the phenomenally popular 1950s *Superman* TV series was made exclusively for kids (and often looked like it had been made *by* children, too.)

It wasn't until the early '60s, when Stan Lee unleashed his stable of new superheroes into the Marvel universe, that comics took a small step out of the children's ghetto and into the world of adolescents. High schoolers and even college students who wouldn't have been caught dead buying DC Comics' juvenile fare were now unashamedly reading about superheroes whose angst-ridden lives made them instantly relatable.

In the late '70s and early '80s, with their *Superman* movies, Warner Brothers at last showed that a superhero property could be adapted for an audience that went far beyond kids and teens. And then, in 1989, Tim Burton's *Batman* movie sealed the deal. But even as late as 1990, when I was working on *Superboy*, there was still some question about who was expected to watch the show—and it wasn't just the prop man who was confused.

Before *Superboy*, I'd had no experience writing superhero stories; the last time I'd so much as looked at a comic book had been more than twenty-five years earlier, when I was thirteen. And the only TV experience I'd had up to the time I started on *Superboy* was in writing and helping to produce cop shows. But that was apparently what *Superboy*'s production company wanted: someone who had the potential to expand the show's audience beyond the children who were already watching, all the way to adults.

It was a risky proposition, because the company was gambling that the show wouldn't turn into something that would accommodate neither children nor adults. They were risking having the show be too old for kids and too young for adults.

Keeping this costly gamble in mind, I began to look for a staff writer... and quickly found that almost all of the candidates weren't taking the show seriously enough. The first writing samples I saw were too light, too silly. Flippant, even. The *characters* could be that way sometimes, but the show itself had to take these characters seriously. They needed to be written as if they were real people with real emotions, even if some of them insisted on wearing their underwear outside their pants.

I finally found a staff writer who was able to take the show seriously while still giving the characters some lightness, but even with his help, and later, the help of a second staff writer, the show never found the expanded audience the executives hoped for. Our episodes were not simple enough for kids, while adults, we figured, couldn't get past the idea of the main character being a boy, even though he was played by actor who was all of 32 years old.

Three years later, I was writing for my first animated show, *Spider-Man*. It ran on the Fox Kids network on Saturday mornings, so there was no question about its intended audience. But every now and then, the writers would slip in a joke or cultural reference that was far over the kids' heads. By and large though, the show was written simply and clearly, the conflict between good and evil was stark, and the show ended up leaving its Saturday morning competition in the dust.

Later, at Warner Bros Animation in 1996, our marching orders were a little different: the animated *Superman* show's primary audience would still be kids, but since it would be running on weekday afternoons, rather than Saturday mornings, we would need to make sure teens and even parents could watch the show and not feel like their intelligence was being insulted. It was a balance that had been admirably struck just a few years earlier by *Batman: The Animated Series*.

Occasionally, but only occasionally, our guest actors would read their lines in exaggerated, cartoonish style, most likely because they'd never seen (or heard) the show, and they figured it would be standard kids' stuff. A handful of those roles had to be recast, but performance tone was never much of a problem when the guest actors had our Batman, Kevin Conroy, to work with in the recording booth. Always serious, and when the occasion called for it, ice cold, Kevin's Batman set the emotional tone for the other actors.

A few years later, during the first season of Warners Animation's *Justice League* TV series, I began to feel the balance shifting in a direction I didn't want it to go. Characters were saying things they didn't need to say in order to make sure our youngest viewers would understand every nuance. Or they'd talk like they were in a cartoon, which was something Warners' writers had always tried to avoid. Before coming to Warners, I'd learned that many old school animation writers had been trained to not rely on animators to make story points with images alone; these writers had been encouraged to "show it <u>and</u> say it," in case the visuals didn't turn out to be clear enough. It was a style that made sure the narrative would be crystal clear to even the youngest viewers.

But judging from the keen, precise work I saw animators at Warners generate, I thought that this precaution was totally unnecessary, and once the *Justice League* series premiered and critical comments started coming in via the Internet, adjustments were made, and the show's second season's dialogue became more adult.

The kiddies' hold on superheroes was loosening in other places, too. In 2005, right after I left Warners Animation to story edit a children's animated Bible show, I met with my old friends at DC Comics in New York to see if they would be interested in putting out a series of comic books based on this new show. "DC doesn't do comics for kids anymore," an executive declared.

Another nail in the kiddie coffin came just a couple of years later, when I was back at Warners Animation, writing a screenplay for a feature-length DVD adaptation of a graphic novel called *Justice League: The New Frontier*. Right from the start, the executives who hired me wanted the feature to be rated PG-13: "Parental guidance: some material may be inappropriate for children under 13."

Thirteen?!! The balance was shifting yet again, and, as it would turn out, a bit too far in the other direction. I was just three years old when I started watching the George Reeves *Superman* TV show, and not much older than that when one of L.A.'s local TV stations started running Max Fleischer's 1940s *Superman* cartoons. I was all of ten when I saw the Batman live-action serials at kiddie matinees, but by age thirteen I had outgrown comic book heroes altogether. If executives like the ones at Warners had been running things when I was a child, there would have been a superhero-sized hole in my cultural growth.

But now, as a writer, I didn't mind the PG-13 at all. I actually welcomed it, because I'd be writing not so much for kids, but more for high school and college students—and quite possibly, a lot of grown men and women. I could have the characters talk like adults, and even have them swear every now and then. I could also make the script's violence just as realistic as it had been in the graphic novel, and the consequences of that violence would be equally realistic. And it would all be adapted to the small screen with nary a censor's note.

There was one other thing, too: I was now taking a step out of the kiddie ghetto. Not a big step; I'd still be kiddie ghetto-adjacent, and it wouldn't be a move that would be noticed by the general public, or even by most TV writers, but among my fellow superhero scribes, it was a big deal.

New Frontier was an unusual experience for that time, but it turned out to be an early stage of a big movement: capes and masks (and externally-worn underwear) were no longer just for kiddies. The same year the *New Frontier* DVD came out, Marvel's ground-breaking *Ironman* live-action feature was released, and it, along with the subsequent *Avengers* movies, pretty much guaranteed that all 'comic book' movies were expected to be mass audience blockbusters from then on. Then in 2019, Warner Brothers broke still more new ground by releasing their *Joker* movie. It was R-rated, which meant that kids under seventeen needed to be accompanied by a parent or guardian to get into the theater.

Back in 2008, just as all this was starting to happen, the *Justice League: The New Frontier* DVD was nominated for an Emmy. The Writers Guild held a reception for all the Emmy-nominated writers that year, and even though *New Frontier* wasn't covered by a Guild contract, the Guild was generous enough to let me in anyway.

At the bar, I found myself standing next to *Mad Men*'s creator, Matthew Weiner. I congratulated him on his nomination—words he'd heard, and would hear, many, many times over the years. Then, obviously as a courtesy, he asked what I had been nominated for.

"It was just an animated thing called *Justice League*," I started to say, and Weiner immediately cut in: "*Justice League*? That's a great show!"

Suddenly the two of us were no longer at a bar in the lobby of the Writers Guild's theater; we were at a high school dance, where Weiner was the prettiest, most popular girl at the school, and I was the ugliest. Someone who had to be escorted to the dance by her brother—her *younger* brother—and whose dress had been hand-sewn by her mother out of burlap. And now, the belle of the ball had taken pity on whatever you'd call her polar opposite and had stepped over to bestow a few kind words on her.

Coming out of that little reverie, I was certain that Matt Weiner wasn't just the nicest person in the Writers Guild—that would've been too low a bar—he was truly the kindest, most generous man in the entire world. And then he said something else I never could have expected: "Could you wait here a minute, please? I want my wife to meet you." Being compassionate to the lowly was one thing, but now he was going too far.

I waited though, and Matt soon brought his wife over to talk to me. It turned out they had four young sons, and one thing the family liked to do together was watch the *Justice League* TV series that I'd helped write a few years earlier. They went on to say they'd even playact along with the episodes, with Weiner taking the role of Superman, his wife playing Wonder Woman, and the sons divvying up the other superheroes among themselves.

Then Matt and his wife started quoting dialogue from *Justice League*'s first season—the very same dialogue that had sometimes made me feel like I was listening to fingernails on a blackboard. So I interrupted them and started talking to them about the more adult season two episodes. Their smiles remained, but their eyes went blank, and it quickly became apparent to me that they hadn't seen any of the later episodes.

When the show stopped being childish, they stopped watching.

END OF CHAPTER

...Except for this: If you've been paying close attention to chronology, you might have some questions about those old Batman serials, and you might also be curious to know how someone my age could have seen them in a movie theater.

There were two Batman serials. The first came out in 1943 and the second in 1949. In the first, the Dynamic Duo's adversary was a Japanese spy called Doctor Daka, who was played by J. Carroll Naish, an American of Irish descent. Need I say more about the casting?

The serial was cheaply produced; the studio couldn't even afford a Batmobile, so Batman and Robin had to make do with a late '30s Cadillac convertible. The second serial didn't have a Batmobile, either; it featured a 1949 Mercury convertible instead, and once again, the writers didn't bother to use any of Batman's extensive rogues' gallery of colorful villains. Instead, they invented a villain called The Wizard. His costume was little more than a black sheet with eyeholes, which looked cheap, but not nearly as cheap as Batman's outfit: long underwear topped by what looked like a costume store's devil mask.

Like the storyline of the first serial, the second's was deadly dull, too: Batman would come close to exposing the Wizard, there'd be some sort of cliffhanging fight, the Wizard would escape, and the next week, Batman would be right back where he started.

There actually were serials from this period that an adult can tolerate watching from beginning to end in a single sitting and not go crazy with boredom -- but not the two Batman serials. Then again, they were never intended to be seen by adults, nor was anyone, not even a child, expected to take in the whole thing in one sitting. Yet somehow, as cheap and unimaginative and boring and repetitive as they were, those two old serials kept playing and playing for years and years at kiddie matinee after kiddie matinee.

How could the little tykes have seen beyond the serials' threadbare production values? Was it that these serials were just about the only superhero movies a kid could see in those days? Or did the cheapness have something to do with their allure? Did it give the kids a sense of superiority, just as those old *Justice League* episodes might have done for the Weiner brood?

Whatever the reasons for the serials' longevity, the first and second Batman serials played in theaters for years. That *Justice League: New Frontier* DVD I worked on should've been so lucky.

POSTSCRIPT: Until I'd done quite a lot of proofreading, I didn't realize that this chapter is structured almost exactly like a movie from the 1940s called *Sullivan's Travels*.

Written and directed by Preston Sturges, *Sullivan's* is about a young director who's had great success making frothy comedies but now feels that it's all been meaningless. He wants to make searing social commentaries, and to do that, this very rich man feels he needs to look at society from the perspective of someone on its lowest rung. So, he leaves his mansion, pretending to be a penniless hobo, and soon finds himself railroaded into prison.

One night, the prison officials run some movies for the convicts, and during a slapstick cartoon, the director looks around at his fellow prisoners, all laughing uproariously, and he suddenly realizes that what people really want—what they need—is just a good laugh every now and then.

So it was with me. Embarrassed because I was writing "kids' stuff," I started to make the material more adult, and in doing so, I lost my original audience.

Sure, you might say, I lost the kids, but didn't the superhero audience grow exponentially? It did, but is that really such a good thing? Try to imagine what the critics in 1943 would have said about a big budget *Batman* or *Captain America* movie, had one been made back then. My guess is, they would have found everything from the costumes to the pre-adolescent power fantasies utterly absurd, and as for the commercial prospects of such films, I doubt that any self-respecting adult would've ever stepped into a theater to see one of them. Yet that's what we have now, millions of adults watching material that at its core is kids' stuff.

A long time ago, I was grousing to a colleague about another colleague's childishness and immaturity.

"Arrested development," my confidante said. "That's what this whole thing's always been about. Didn't you know that?"

STAN BERKOWITZ

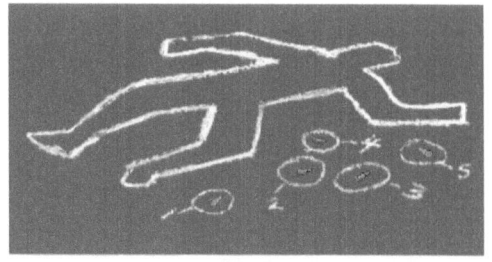

CHAPTER SEVEN
"DAMMIT, HOOKER, SHE WAS MY NIECE!"

Even without context, that line sounds unnatural and badly compromised, doesn't it? And it actually was a compromise. It was supposed to be a reference to a daughter, of course, and how a daughter became a niece isn't just a tale of the pitfalls of episodic TV or the whims of executives, it's also about what can happen on a Friday afternoon, when everyone just wants to go home.

When *TJ Hooker* premiered on ABC, I was in my early thirties, still working at a day job, but ready to quit and write for TV the minute my agent could come up with anything. Or rather, almost anything. One day she called to tell me she had a contact at *Hooker*, and if I could work out some script ideas, she'd set up a pitch meeting for me. She sent me some sample stories from the show, but after reading them, I came up dry. Couldn't think of a single story.

The show focused on a small group of policemen led by William Shatner. They were uniformed street cops, but they functioned more like detectives, busting major crimes and tracking down psychos and criminal masterminds alike. And at least one of the lead characters would have to have some kind of personal connection to that week's case.

It was a world that didn't seem real to me, and I couldn't comprehend its rules. And, since preparing for a pitch meeting takes lots of time and effort, I was pretty sure mine would be wasted.

There was another issue, too. *Hooker* was an old school TV series, anthological in the sense that each episode's story was separate from the other episodes' stories. You didn't need to see last week's show in order to understand this week's. The weakness of such a format is that by its nature, it can't very realistic. That's because in the real world, a cop doesn't get involved in gunplay every week. Some cops even go through whole careers without having to draw their weapons. Were they living in the real world, *Hooker*'s cops would have been assigned permanent desk duty after just a couple of shootings.

BEYOND THE BAT

If not realism, then what was the show selling? Reassurance, I think. Each episode began with some kind of threat to order, and by the end, order was restored by the good people who were the show's regulars. You could sleep well after watching *TJ Hooker*.

The same could be said about lots of shows from that era, but over at NBC, there were a couple of series whose creators seemed more willing to rattle our cages. *Hill Street Blues* was a cop show, but with ongoing stories, like a soap opera, and it focused on the serio-comic quirks of its large cast of characters. *Miami Vice* was essentially anthological, but thanks to its use of contemporary music, its avant-garde fashion sense and its glamorization of the drug culture, it seemed anything but old school. It was shows like these that I watched regularly and were closer to my sensibility than *TJ Hooker*. So, unlike a real pro, I told my agent I couldn't pitch to *Hooker*.

Somehow, I didn't suffer much from this lack of professionalism, and within just a couple of years, I had a new agent and was finally able to quit my day job and go to work on the *Mike Hammer* show at Columbia Pictures TV—where *TJ Hooker* was also being filmed.

After I'd spent just three weeks on *Hammer*, the writing staff as well as the cast and crew got catastrophic news: our star, Stacy Keach, had been busted for cocaine possession while visiting England months earlier, and he had just made the mistake of returning there for what he expected to be a mild judicial wrist-slapping. What he got instead was a six-month jail sentence that began almost the minute the verdict came in. So, with Christmas just a week away, the studio was forced to send everyone home—cast, crew, writers, everyone.

"But I have a contract," I whined to my new agent.

"They're claiming it was an act of God," he replied matter-of-factly.

"God made Stacy Keach bring coke into England?" I asked.

The agent patiently explained that the relative pittance the studio still owed on my contract would be easy for them to give me, but if they did, they'd have to pay everyone else too, and that was obviously out of the question.

Determined not to tuck my tail between my legs and ask for my day job back, I managed to get a script assignment on a series about a group of spies. But that script was long-completed by the time Memorial Day rolled around, and I was again looking for a job. Fortunately, my agent had gone back to Columbia to bring up the act of God thing again. He pointed out to them that instead of a lawsuit, the matter could be settled amicably—if Columbia were to hire me again.

And it just so happened they had an opening for a staff writer on another of their shows: *TJ Hooker*. Yes, the same show for which I'd come up dry just a couple of years earlier. But now, I was a seasoned pro who had all of six months' experience under his belt… and needed a job. I wouldn't be coming up dry again.

I showed up at the studio brimming with enthusiasm, but quickly realized no one cared. What was a step up for me was a step down for almost everyone else there. That was because ABC had canceled *TJ Hooker* at the end of the previous season, with the series still one season short of enough episodes for a full syndication package. Desperate to get that final season, Columbia convinced CBS to pick it up.

But CBS wasn't going to schedule it in primetime. Instead, it would be airing in the 11:30 PM slot and, not surprisingly, it would be shot on a much lower budget than previous seasons. Columbia would get its syndication package, but for the creative team, this might as well have been Siberia. They'd be getting less money, and the show had no chance of renewal, so everyone was guaranteed to be out on the street in February or March of the following year, with their most recent credit not even having been in prime time.

If there was one good thing about any of this, it was that the late-night slot offered an opportunity to write darker, more adult stories than could be presented at 8 PM on a Saturday evening. Or so I thought.

STAN BERKOWITZ

Soon after I was hired, I got a quick rundown from the supervising producer on how not to write for William Shatner. Don't get him wet, I was told, it's a hassle for hair and makeup, and Bill doesn't like it either. Don't sit him down in a scene, because it'll sap his energy. And don't put exclamation marks in his dialogue, because he'll put too much energy into the line. There was one other rule, but I wouldn't find out about that one until much later.

As it turned out, I didn't really need to know any of those rules. That was because a veteran producer slotted just below the supervising producer would end up doing most of the writing and rewriting himself. So, the other staff writer and I were usually left to spend our days at the office looking for typos in the scripts or rummaging through videos of past seasons' episodes to find car chases that could be dropped into new episodes in order to keep costs down. Only on very rare occasions were we allowed to write or rewrite so much as a line or two of dialogue.

Before I came aboard, freelancers had pitched script ideas to the bosses. Several had been approved by the studio and network, and while I watched old episodes, the freelancers were already at work turning their pitches into scripts.

One of the pitches was inspired by the movie *Hardcore*, which had come out a few years earlier and starred George C. Scott as a mid-western businessman who makes a grim journey to Los Angeles in an attempt to pull his wayward daughter out of the porn business.

Being "inspired" by a movie (or book or news item) was not all that unusual in the episodic TV world. Six months earlier, that script I wrote for the spy show had been "inspired" by Ian Fleming's *Casino Royale* (the book, not the movie; the 1967 film bore no resemblance to Fleming's story, and the Daniel Craig version wasn't even a glimmer in anyone's eye at that point.)

My script had a secret agent try to bankrupt a rich bad guy during a high stakes card game. That's the basic plot of *Casino Royale*, so, to make my story a slightly less obvious theft, I set it on a cruise ship, added some characters who were working at cross-purposes, and then threw in a couple of murders. The confined setting and the multiple corpses gave the script a whiff of Agatha Christie, and the resulting mixture was different enough from both "inspirations" so that no hackles were raised.

Had the writer of our *Hardcore* episode directly adapted that movie's storyline to *TJ Hooker*, it would have been too obvious a theft, and also, there wouldn't have been much for Hooker to do in it, not unless he was going to be the father of the porn actress, and nobody on the show would have entertained that thought for even an instant.

So, just as I and so many other writers had done, this freelancer added a second "inspiration": in this case, snuff films. These were amateur movies, exhibited clandestinely and supposedly showing people actually being sadistically murdered on-screen during sex acts. Did such films really exist? There was much debate about that at the time, leading many to wonder who would be stupid enough to film himself committing a capital crime. Even so, the subject briefly flitted across the headlines back in the eighties, before sinking into obscurity.

The episode's victim would be the daughter of an older cop who had been Hooker's mentor on the force. That would be the required personal connection to the case, and a can of film would be the episode's MacGuffin. Hooker and his pals would have two important things to do: catch the killer with the celluloid evidence in hand, and also, prevent the old cop from going rogue and murdering his daughter's killer.

There would be no deep dive into the porn world and no questions about how some people could be so fucked up that they'd get off watching a young girl sadistically murdered. The barest bones of the story didn't even involve sex; at its core, it was about the guilt a father felt over the depths to which his daughter had fallen. And then there was the major role reversal of a younger man (Hooker) giving an older man a lesson in what it meant to be a good cop.

That's pretty much the script that was circulated a few days before preparation for shooting was to begin. The other staff writer and I had a few trivial notes, but the supervising producer—essentially the showrunner—did have one note that would prove to be significant.

"Bill works best with younger guest stars, in their early forties," he informed us. (Shatner was fifty-four).

So, the older cop would now be a younger cop.

Did this note actually originate with our supervising producer? Hard to say; his office wasn't in the same building as the other writers' offices, and we didn't have daily contact with him. But he was certainly in the loop, which meant that he would have known for weeks that this episode was going to partner Shatner with an older actor. So why did he wait so long to ask for the change?

My guess is that the request came from Shatner himself. Shatner was not part of the writing department, so he normally wouldn't see a script until about week before it was going to go into production—which was right about the time the supervising producer told us to make the guest lead a lot younger.

If this was Shatner's request, it brings up an interesting conundrum: At fifty-four, Shatner had three adult children, but he was playing a character who was maybe ten years younger, and the father of a pre-adolescent child. Did he think that sharing the screen with an older actor would make him look older? Probably, though couldn't it also be true that if you appear with people who are younger than you, that could make you look even older? As I noted, it's a conundrum, and the solution was to simply do as requested and rewrite the script for a younger actor.

No problem, I thought. The only thing that would change would be the mentoring element. Instead of the turnabout of the student getting the teacher back on the right path, it would now be the teacher mentoring the student — yet again. A small loss, I felt, and more than compensated for by the promised chemistry between our star and his younger guest star. An hour's-worth of rewriting at most.

And then the bombshell: we were told by the supervising producer that if our intended father was only in his early forties, he couldn't possibly be old enough to have a daughter who'd gotten involved in the porn world. Huh?

Surprised, we appealed, using simple arithmetic to make our case: she's maybe twenty, he's forty-two — couldn't he have had her when he was twenty-two? Nope, we were told, he couldn't. Appeal denied.

Just guessing, but the concern might have been Hooker's age again. If a younger man had a daughter who was significantly older than Hooker's kid, mightn't it seem a little odd? Mightn't it shine an unwanted light on Hooker's age? Mightn't some viewers, somewhere, ask why the younger man has a child who's older than the older man's? Unlikely, but not impossible, so why even let the question be asked? Most viewers, I'm sure, wouldn't have noticed or cared, but there was at least one party whose appearance of youth was certainly very important to him.

The supervising producer's solution was to make our forty-two-year-old guest star the girl's uncle. That would certainly be a far weaker relationship than father-daughter, so the ties would have to be bolstered as best we could. The cop's sister would be a single mother, and the cop stepped in at an early age to act as a surrogate father.

Did he eventually gain a wife and kids of his own? Not mentioned. Did he sacrifice his own potential family because he was so busy helping to raise his niece? Also not mentioned. Could that mean his obsession with his niece was an indication his feelings for her were more than avuncular? That possibility, like the possibility of her being Hooker's daughter, was never considered.

When the old cop was about to go rogue, his big confrontation with Hooker featured the line, "Dammit, Hooker, she was my daughter!" That line now had to be changed to "Dammit, Hooker, she was my niece!"

(In retrospect, maybe "She was *like* a daughter to me," or "She was family!" would have been a little easier on the ears, but whatever the case, I heard myself muttering to the other staff writer, "Dammit, Hooker, she was my ex-fiancée's second cousin's foster child.")

With all the changes made, the snuff film script went into prep. Over the course of an uneventful week, the episode's director scouted locations, sat in at casting sessions, worked on a shooting schedule and gave a few script notes. An actor in his early forties was duly hired as the guest star, and all the rest of prep went smoothly, right up to Friday afternoon, the last day of prep, when a call came in for our producer. It was from the network representative.

It so happened that the rep who kept his eye on *TJ Hooker* was a former actor named Dwayne Hickman, who'd once played Dobie Gillis on TV. Now he was an executive at CBS, and he was calling to tell the producer he had a problem with the snuff film script.

"You can't do a snuff-film story," he said.

The producer was in his late sixties, and though that was his title, he didn't get involved in casting, location scouts, editing or even watching dailies. All he did was sit in his office and write and re-write scripts. Age had less to do with that than attitude; he avoided contact with his colleagues as much as he could because he hated us all.

Surly even on a good day, he always ate lunch alone in this office while reading a newspaper. No Hollywood lunches for him! His staff writers were a nuisance to him, and his supervising producer boss was talentless. He had a hearing aid but seldom used it—and not because of discomfort or vanity. It was mostly because he didn't want to hear a thing any of us had to say.

I figured he sensed—correctly, as it turned out—that this would be his last job after 30 very productive years, including a long stint on *Fantasy Island*, which was one of the few things he talked about—along with his gun collection—that seemed to make him happy. Now he was facing a future where there would be no retirement party, no awards and no gold watch. Only a phone that would never ring again.

At that moment, though, he didn't let his attitude get in the way of his professionalism. He somehow stayed calm as he reminded Hickman that weeks earlier, the network had approved the premise and the outline, neither of which made any secret of the snuff film element. Also, it was too late in the prep process for us to pull this script and substitute another. None of that made a dent, though. We couldn't do a snuff film episode, not even for an 11:30 PM slot.

In defense of the network (a phrase seldom written), the decision probably wasn't as much of an ill-timed whim as it seemed. Maybe Hickman had been busy on other shows, or maybe he was new to this assignment. Maybe he'd been okay with the idea, but one of his bosses belatedly stepped in to nix it.

Whatever the reason, though, it looked like we were majorly screwed.

It seemed as if our only alternative would be a very expensive one: shut down production for a week and prep a new script… while continuing to pay the whole crew their weekly wages. While I was fretting about that, the producer was looking off into space and thinking. After what seemed like just a few seconds, he told us what was going to happen to the snuff film story.

At the beginning, the girl would still be killed on camera, but it wouldn't be on purpose, it would be an accident. In mid-take, she would tell her co-star (who was also producing this porn film) that she didn't want to do porn any more. Her conscience was getting to her. Camera still running, her frustrated co-star would start pushing and slapping her. She would fall back, hit her head on a prop and die on camera.

"But then it wouldn't be murder," I said.

The producer, who had once been a cop, said that if someone happens to die during the commission of a felony, it's considered murder.

"Making porn's not a felony anymore," I countered.

"It is if the girl's under eighteen," he replied with a rare twinkle.

Saved! Only a few lines needed to be changed, and then off to production it went. But wait, now that the girl was going to be that young, did her uncle still have to be her uncle? Now there'd be a twenty-five-year age gap between them; couldn't she go back to being his daughter? And couldn't we finally get rid of that awful "niece" line?

If that thought occurred to anyone after everything we'd been through that day, no one mentioned it. It was, after all, Friday night.

STAN BERKOWITZ

CHAPTER EIGHT
RACISM AND ME

I hadn't even started writing the script, yet the director and I were already scouting locations in his old Buick—that's how eager he was to make his movie. As we drove farther and farther north into L.A.'s San Fernando Valley, he reached for the radio and asked, "Mind if I listen to Rush?" "The band?" I asked. "Limbaugh," he replied.

Right then, I should've known things were going to end badly.

We were looking for a small plaza or mini-mall that would be the movie's main location, a stand-in for an actual mini-mall the director had been telling me about. A gang of drug dealers had turned it into a drive-through pharmaceuticals mart, and the merchants who tried to do something about it were beaten or had their stores vandalized. Whenever the police were called, the gang members always scattered "like cockroaches" — a simile courtesy of the director, who was so incensed by this utter lawlessness he decided to produce and direct a movie about it. But his movie wasn't going to be a documentary; it would be something up Limbaugh's alley, a piece of wish fulfillment about a tough ex-cop who comes to town and cleans up the mini-mall using a method the director remembered from his youth in 1940s Pittsburgh: street corner justice. No mere relic of the past, that kind of so-called justice is still around; just ask George Floyd's relatives.

But the director wasn't going to go anywhere near an indictment of police brutality; he wanted to shoot an urban vigilante flick in the *Death Wish* mold. Making it a little different would be that the ex-cop wouldn't be a loner; he would assemble a group of former felons he'd busted to help him. Sort of a Dirty Half-Dozen. Would that alone make the movie different enough from all the other urban vigilante movies that had gone before?

I thought it would need another element to make it stand out, so I began to consider something an actor friend once told me. This actor had been raised in Puerto Rico and was now making a good part of his living doing Spanish-language voiceovers. He'd told me that for each job, he had to accent his Spanish differently; for ads and promos that ran in Miami, for example, he would put on a Cuban accent. For the

New York market, his accent would be Puerto Rican, and for Los Angeles, Mexican.

I wondered what would be so wrong about using, say, a Mexican accent for a Miami promo. "The audience would reject it. They don't like each other," he explained. Keeping that in mind, I began to think about exploiting a rift like that in our movie-to-be. What if the first group of drug dealers our hero encounters were Chicanos—American-born kids of Mexican descent who'd grown up in the neighborhood and were now eking out a living in the drug business? And what if they were fighting a turf war against a far more brutal group of recent immigrants from Central America?

That element was in my first draft of the script -- which would be the only draft I'd do. Not nasty enough or dirty enough, the director told me. So he brought in another writer, and when he was happy with a new draft -- presumably one that was nasty and dirty enough—he sent it to me.

The main thing I noticed about this new draft was that the storyline now had an almost circular quality. The drug dealers would do something bad, the hero and his friends would retaliate, and then the bad guys would do something else. And so on, without escalation—just a cycle of provocation and retaliation. The individual scenes were structured that way too, with insults leading only to more insults, threats to more threats, and no modulation of tone. I took it as a sign of the director's seething outrage, which wasn't modulated, either.

"How did he handle the drug dealers?" a mutual friend soon inquired.

I asked this friend if he'd ever seen the movie *Zulu*. The friend laughed; *Zulu*'s climactic scene had British soldiers shooting wave after wave of Zulu warriors, leaving heaps of undifferentiated bodies twitching all over the battlefield.

"You're saying he denied the drug dealers their humanity?" the friend asked, summing it up better than I could.

The new draft of the script had no culture clash between the dealers and no individuation of them. Every one of the dealers was irredeemably evil, and that was as subtle as it got.

Shooting began in February of 1994. I was working on something else by then, but I was going to slip away once a week to watch them shoot. I was able to get in just one visit to the set before production was shut down.

The director had started shooting before all his financing was in place, and just a week into it, one of his financing partners dropped out. Shooting had to stop, but the director's outrage wasn't going to let him give up that easily.

A few weeks after the plug was pulled, he invited me to a screening room to see the edited footage from his week of shooting. There wasn't much, but he seemed quite proud of what there was. I didn't find it all compelling, and as the lights came up, I wondered why he would care what I thought of it. I was just a writer, and one who'd been substantially rewritten at that. But the director cared plenty about what I thought of his footage. It was because he needed an investor to help him finish the film. Me.

At that point, I did have money, but I had even more of something else: incredible, blind luck.

Back when I started writing my draft of the script, I was about to be married, and I decided to write a part for my wife-to-be. It was a substantial supporting role that would've made good use of her physicality. She was an athlete, she'd acted in a dozen or so action flicks, and I was certain she'd be perfect for this one. And despite the heavy rewriting, the part I wrote for her was still largely intact. But when it came time to cast the part, did the director even think of bringing her in to read for it? Nope. Was I angry about that? Of course.

But now, months later, when the director was asking me to invest, I began to contemplate what might've been, and how lucky I was. What if she *had* gotten the part and *had* appeared in that first week's footage? I would be in an impossible position: trying to choose between supporting my wife's acting career or holding onto a good chunk of my life savings by not investing in a movie I was certain would never make a cent.

But thanks to the director not casting her, I was free of that particular obligation to her career. And I certainly had no obligation to him or his film, either. So, I just told him I was saving my money for a house and walked out of the screening room, life savings intact.

Somehow, somewhere, the director eventually got the money he needed to finish his film, and a year later, my bride and I joined him and several other cast and crew members to watch the movie.

It begins in Pittsburgh with a rape scene that was supposed to be stomach-turning, but the actor who played the rapist was Clint Howard, a small, round fellow who looked like he would have been more at home in a movie featuring my new wife's childhood favorites, Larry, Moe and Curly—The Three Stooges. But as the scene unfolded, I could feel my wife shaking in the next seat. Could this sequence have struck a nerve? I leaned over to see if she was all right... and quickly realized she was convulsing with barely suppressed laughter. "She's being raped by _Larry_," she whispered.

It got worse from there.

In reading the revised script, I hadn't paid much attention to its ethnic stereotypes; you don't really notice accents until you actually hear them, and as the film ran on, there were plenty of accents to hear. The Mexican/cholo accents were expected, of course, but what I'd forgotten was the polyglot nature of the other characters. There was the humble Asian donut maker, the Bible-spouting Black ex-con, the old Jewish jeweler who talked like dis because he vas from de old country (and was portrayed by an actor who was from a very old country -- England -- and who was all of nine years older than me), and of course there had to be a Catholic priest who couldn't be from anywhere other than Ireland (and who was played by a young Bryan Cranston).

Amid the cacophony of fake accents, I remembered our friend's remark about denial of humanity and found myself wondering what is racism, if not this very thing? Being unable to think beyond stereotypes? Check. Assuming that certain ethnicities have a natural inclination toward crime? Check. And believing that a certain other ethnicity should be the one that saves everyone and restores order? This thing checked all the boxes.

I grew up in a nearly all-white section of the San Fernando Valley. My one Chicano friend was so thoroughly assimilated, he couldn't speak a word of his parents' native language until he started taking Spanish classes in high school. And as for Blacks, I never had a class with even one until I left the Valley to go to UCLA.

The civil rights struggle was one of the major news stories of my childhood (and my dotage, too, as well as everything in between) so it wasn't as if I was unaware of racism. In the movies and TV shows of my childhood, mean old racist characters would usually end up having their lives saved by selfless Negro doctors or soldiers, and then slink off to mend their evil ways. In real life, though, the outspoken racists I knew never had a comeuppance, and because of what I'd seen in the movies, and because these people were my classmates and neighbors and I had to see them every day, I found myself giving them the benefit of the doubt by viewing their racism, and racism in general, as just a quirk or kink, or even a bad habit that otherwise decent people might have.

But sitting in that screening room, with our friend's "denial of humanity" remark echoing in my mind, I began to wonder if racism might not be just a kink, but rather, a symptom of a more generalized disorder. I asked myself if someone who denies the humanity of minorities is likely to also be the kind of person who denies everyone else's humanity.

When the director first approached me about writing the script, I told him that Writers Guild rules would require his new production company to sign a deal with the Guild if he wanted to hire me. So, his little company soon signed with the Guild, and that brought up the matter of my compensation. All I wanted was Guild minimum for a low budget feature ($25,000 in those days), but the director didn't even have that much. He would have it, he assured me, once the money for production came in, on the first day of shooting.

No problem, I said. I had money in the bank, nothing else to do at that moment, and no reason not trust him. True, I hadn't had much personal contact with him until then, but he had directed several episodes of syndicated cop shows I'd written, they'd gone smoothly and hadn't offended anyone, and he came highly recommended by that mutual friend of ours.

Soon after the rewrite was completed, the director got his production money. But there was less than he hoped for, he told me, and he still couldn't pay me. But if I signed a new contract which would allow him to pay me when he made a distribution deal, he would double my compensation to $50,000.

Yeah, I know, I shouldn't have gone along with it, but what if I had insisted on the $25,000 just as he was about to start shooting? A lawyer would have certainly gobbled up most of my money, had I'd gotten any, and had I asked my agent or the Writers Guild to help, all they could have done was make threats about him never working in this town again. But what would he have cared about that? He was in his late fifties and on a kamikaze mission to rid America's mini-malls of the scourge of Mexican drug dealers. He would've kept right on shooting. So, I agreed to this new deal, and, as expected, I didn't get the $50,000, either. I figured it was because the director was never able to make a distribution deal, but a few years later, when the movie showed up on cable as part of just such a deal, I finally went to the Writers Guild for an arbitration.

My name was stuck on a bad movie that no one went to see, and I had nothing other than that to show for the time I'd spent on the script. Had the film been any good, or at least not embarrassing, I probably wouldn't have asked for an arbitration. But I, and everybody else who'd worked on it, had been treated so high-handedly by this director, I figured he should be held to account and made to pay up.

No one from the director's long-dormant production company bothered to show up for the arbitration, so it went smoothly, and in my favor. At the end, I wanted to know how soon it would be before I got my $50,000.

It was only then that the arbitrator explained that the Guild didn't have the money, nor had the director's production company put anything into any kind of escrow account. I was told that if I wanted the money, I would now have to go to civil court and sue. Then what had been the point of the arbitration, I wanted to know. All it was designed to do was help me make a stronger case when I sued, the arbitrator said. But exactly who would I sue? The director's now-penniless production company? I certainly couldn't sue the director, who incorporated the company and ran it into the ground; he would always be protected by that corporate shell.

All the Guild could do was put companies like the director's on its so-called strike list, which would've prevented Guild writers from ever working for him again. But by this point he was long-gone from Hollywood, raising horses somewhere and presumably avoiding mini-malls.

Novice writers always worry about producers cheating them, but over a very long career, it's only happened to me a few times, and never was the culprit someone who just wanted to save himself some money. It's always been more like the case of this director, when it was someone who believed in his project so much, he was willing to make risky business decisions in order to get it in front of the public. When the gamble didn't pay off, it was just too bad for everyone involved.

Whatever the motivation for the screwing, though, I was far from alone. As best as I could tell, the only people who got anything back from the distribution deal were the ones who actually put up production money. The rest of us—actors, crewmen and writers, who only invested time and labor—we all got stiffed. As for the director, he didn't get much, either. No money, a poorly reviewed cap to an otherwise estimable career, no more movies to direct, and above all, the well-earned enmity of those who worked with him at the end of his career.

It was almost as if he had wanted it all to happen; he'd consistently made one bad decision after another, and not just when it came to this final film of his. Over the years there'd been bad marriages, fights with studio executives — not just arguments, actual fights — and lots more. He'd littered his life with far too much of this sort of thing for it to have been purely a matter of chance. Did he have some kind of deep-seated self-destructive impulse? I realized — too late -- that he must have. When someone denies everyone else their humanity, mightn't it stem from having too little of his own?

POSTSCRIPT: Soon after I finished writing this chapter, the director died of Covid 19. I hadn't seen or heard from him in over twenty years, but I find it impossible not to imagine him continuing to listen to Rush (Limbaugh, not the band) right up to the end, even as Limbaugh ranted about the virus being a hoax.

Just a few months after the director died, Limbaugh died, too, though not from Covid. But does it really matter what killed the two of them? The timing of their deaths was close to perfect: right in the middle of the Black Lives Matter movement, something neither man could have had much sympathy for. Do their deaths have any kind of symbolic value? Could they be an indication of the end of an era? Specifically, the end of racism?

Only in the movies, I'm afraid.

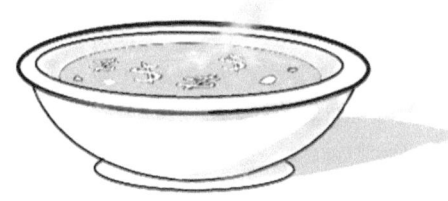

CHAPTER NINE
THE HALF-MILLION-DOLLAR BOWL OF SOUP

The president was talking about my show! Well, it wasn't really *my* show, I was just the story editor. And it wasn't the show he was actually talking about; it was the comic book the show was based on. But it really was the president—Barack Hussein Obama himself. And that's when all the trouble started.

The animation director I'd worked with on *Friends and Heroes* had been hired to direct a new comic book-based superhero series, and he'd recommended me for the story editor position—basically, head writer.

"It's called *THE 99*," he said, "and it's about Islamic superheroes."

Curious to see what a mixture of capes, tights and Islam would look like, I hurried to a comics store and picked up some early issues of the comic. They looked good: extra-large pages, high-quality paper, bright colors—and all in English, written by American writers. But where was the Islam?

The first character you meet is a blond American kid who lives in St. Louis. He's a paraplegic called Wheeler, and I wondered if he was supposed to be a Muslim. Could've been, but his religion--if he even has one--is never mentioned. Soon, Wheeler meets some Middle Easterners—Muslims, I assumed, but again, there's no mention of religion.

What they do mention to Wheeler is the origin of 99 gemstones they call the Noor stones. They tell Wheeler that back in Baghdad in the thirteenth century, there was a huge library that came under attack from an invading army. Fearing for the safety of the books, the local scholars and alchemists invented the Noor stones as a way of preserving the power in all those words.

When the invaders dumped the books into the Tigris River in order to use their bulk as a bridge, the Noor stones were bathed in the ink that washed off the pages of the books, and that miraculously gave each stone a unique super-power.

Powers that came from words written in books? What writer wouldn't be hooked by that? I certainly was, and after a brief, painless negotiation, I signed

BEYOND THE BAT

on as story editor. Soon after, I met Naif al-Mutawa, the creator of *THE 99*. He was a Kuwaiti psychologist who'd spent a lot of his youth in New York, and was now the father of four young sons. He wanted to do something that wasn't very fashionable in 2008: he was going to make comic books and cartoons for kids. And, with his close ties to New York, he'd been emotionally scarred by the 9/11 attacks, so his other mission was to present Middle Easterners as positive role models.

I almost wrote "Muslims" in that last sentence, but that wouldn't have been accurate, because never in the comics, and never in any of the fifty-two animated episodes I'd go on to story edit, were the words "Muslim" or "Islam" ever uttered. This was by design; the mainstream comics of Naif's youth didn't talk about religion, so why should his own? All it could do was alienate many readers, especially Westerners.

But Naif didn't entirely ignore the religious tradition into which he'd been born. Remember those Noor stones? There happened to be 99 of them, and not at all coincidentally, Islam lists 99 names for Allah. So, the comic's writers were tasked with finding superhero-style powers to go with many of those names.

For example, name number 91 is Ad Dharr, which may be translated as "the distressor," and in the hands of the writers of the comic books, that became the power to generate intense pain. Wheeler, the American paraplegic (who would be called "Weller" in the TV series) had found that particular stone, and simply by pointing at people, he could rack them with pain.

Similarly, a kid from Saudi Arabia named Nawaf became the huge and immensely powerful Jabbar, thanks to a Noor stone associated with name #9, "the compellor" or "the restorer." There was also a woman called Batina—"the hidden one"—whose superpower was invisibility, and who wore a full niqab—a total body covering with just an open slit for her eyes. As such, she was one of just a few of *THE 99*'s characters who was clearly identifiable as a Muslim. Many of the rest, but not all of them, did come from Middle Eastern and/or Muslim majority countries, but their religion(s) was never explicitly stated.

The plan was to have one hero per country, which we hoped would allow the comics and the TV series to acquire an international fan base. To achieve this, the series would need to be an inoffensive guest in even the most religious households... which meant that the writers would have to go beyond the usual children's broadcast standards that pertained to sex and violence.

And that didn't just mean no pork chops, no dogs (considered unclean in many parts of the Muslim world) and no sex or even light romance—even though many of our characters were teens or young adults. There were other, less familiar taboos our TV writers had to work around.

One writer innocently set up an ambush sequence in which two of the heroes, a male and a female, were inside the back of a truck, lying in wait for the bad guys. Nothing was going to happen between them while they were in there, but nevertheless, Naif raised a red flag, because unmarried males and females aren't supposed to be alone together. The easy solution was to add a third hero to the hiding place, something that raised a question among a few of the writers: hadn't these people ever heard of threesomes?

As the final version of the scene played out, no one would have guessed that there'd been any kind of problem. And so it was with the rest of the restrictions. We didn't want the viewers—whether in Morocco or Mississippi—to feel that anything had been cut out or censored, even though the writers needed to be very, very sensitive to certain cultural issues.

To help with this, I tried to locate Muslim writers, but neither the Writers Guild of America nor the Writers Guild of Canada were of any use, and when I told Naif what I was trying to do, he said not to worry about it, and just hire the best writers I could find. So, I did (and just a few years later, both Guilds were—and still are—offering vastly improved diversity programs).

Scripting for *THE 99* TV series began in late 2008, with writer Henry Gilroy giving up his Christmas and New Year to write a four-episode (two-hour) pilot.

Around that same time, the Discovery Channel was teaming up with the Hasbro toy company to create a new cable channel they called The Hub. There were already 24-hour kids cable channels out there—Disney and Nickelodeon, to name two of the biggest—so The Hub's mission would be to attract a slightly different audience: families. They would run shows that kids liked, but could also be watched by parents who wouldn't feel as though their intelligence was being insulted. A prime example: reruns of the *Batman Beyond* series I'd helped write ten years earlier.

Heading The Hub would be Margaret Loesch, a veteran children's TV executive who had run the Fox Kids operation when I was writing for *Spider-Man* during the mid-1990s. Assuming that The Hub would need family-friendly programming, I suggested to Naif that he should contact Margaret. And just like that, a deal was made.

Going on little more than the comics and Henry's as-yet unproduced pilot script, Margaret bought *THE 99* for The Hub. By the standards of the day, it wasn't a great deal for Naif: about $20,000 per episode to run the first twenty-six. Though the episodes would cost far more than that to produce—around $250,000 per–
–no one on *THE 99*'s side of the bargaining table was

complaining. That was because the deal allowed *THE 99*'s company to get whatever compensation it could from running the show everywhere else in the world.

And now, with an American network ready to run the series, *THE 99* had a crucial piece of its marketing strategy in place: a deal with an American cable outlet, something that gives a show considerable credibility in the rest of the world. And even if *THE 99* couldn't recoup its entire budget from the international TV market, there were still merchandising deals to be made: with 99 potential action figures, and each one's origin in a different country, the opportunities for toy sales seemed almost limitless.

As executives from the show's UK-based production company set out across the globe to make more TV deals, the Los Angeles-based writers and I continued to generate scripts, while the animators, based in the United Kingdom and India, were bringing these scripts to life. The show was being rendered entirely in computer animation, which is vastly different from so-called 2-D animation.

For years, a writer's consolation for working in animation, as opposed to the more adult live-action, had been that anything that can be drawn on paper can be animated, and the only limitation was the writer's imagination, not the show's budget. Computer animation (or 3-D) is different. Its characters and sets need to be "built"—not physically, but rather, inside computers. And that work isn't easy.

In fact, just as live-action writers might be told by producers that their scripts require too many locations or too many characters, a writer working on a computer-animated show (as most are now) might hear the very same thing: too many characters, too many sets to build. It seemed like the same amount of time and labor that went into building a set for a live-action show also went into creating a set that would exist only inside a computer.

For the writers, the 2-D to 3-D transition was not easy, but once the limitations were established, scripting went relatively smoothly. Like 2-D animation, however, 3-D was a slow process, and once a script was written, an episode might take as much as half a year to animate.

During those months, Naif was not idle. Beside keeping a watchful eye on our scripts, he was doing what he could to raise the *THE 99*'s profile. He did a Ted Talk and also participated in a PBS documentary about the property (*Wham Bam Islam*). And then there was that time he met President Obama.

It was during a presidential summit on entrepreneurship, and as Naif sat in the audience, Obama talked about *THE 99*'s heroes embodying "the teachings and tolerance of Islam." Naif can still be seen on YouTube, beaming as Obama talks about *THE*

99. And I beamed, too, when I heard about the shout-out.

The last shout-out for any project I'd worked on had been ten or twelve years earlier, and the person doing the shouting was Howard Stern. But now it was April, 2010, The Hub was scheduled to make its debut in just a few months, and soon after, *THE 99* would premiere in America.

I was ecstatic. Could there have been any better publicity than this? My only worry was that when the show premiered sometime in the fall, it might not live up to its presidential hype. I needn't have worried though, because the show would never premiere.

What I and everyone else had forgotten was that 2010 was an election year—not a presidential election, but one in which a third of the Senate and the entire House of Representatives were up for grabs, and, despite being an affable middle-of-the-roader, Obama was hated by a lot of people, most notably Rupert Murdoch, who owned both the Fox network and the *New York Post* newspaper.

Almost immediately after the election of 2008, Obama had utilized slim Democratic majorities in the House and Senate to pass a landmark health insurance bill, and right wingers like Murdoch wanted to make sure the November, 2010 elections would deprive Obama of those majorities, so he couldn't pass any more progressive legislation. With their mission clearly delineated, Murdoch's minions set out to look for things they could use as sticks to beat Obama with.

One such stick was Obama's apparent endorsement of our TV series, and a *New York Post* columnist named Andrea Peyser dutifully wrote a piece about it that was timed to appear just three weeks before the election. In it, she wrote about Obama's shout-out and condemned the show as Islamic propaganda. Then she urged The Hub not to run it.

Judging from Peyser's comments, it was clear she'd never seen the show — she couldn't have, it hadn't aired yet—but her sentiments were not so easily dismissed. In most instances, this kind of controversy would be good publicity, but not in the world of kids TV, where executives don't want to run the risk of offending even a single viewer.

In response to Peyser's column, The Hub pushed back *THE 99*'s premiere, then pushed it back again and again, while at the same time, impressive-looking episodes were coming back from the production team — episodes for which some of the writers had done the best work of their careers. But it would turn out to be work that would never be seen by a mass audience.

That November, Obama lost his congressional majority, and along with it, most of his plans for progressive legislation. Then, after months of postponements, The Hub's executives finally told us that if we got an offer from another network, they wouldn't mind at all if we took it. And we could even keep The Hub's $500,000 advance.

But Peyser had poisoned the well, and there were no other offers from American outlets. Nothing from Europe, either, though the show did find some outlets in Asia and the Middle East and later, on Facebook. There would be no toy deals, and all told, Naif's investors would lose millions. Yet a financial loss might not have been the worst of it. In 2014, four years after *THE 99* was supposed to premiere on The Hub, Naif was sued by a man in Kuwait—for blasphemy.

Naif had tried hard not to offend any Muslims who might watch *THE 99*, but there was nothing he could do about his creation's central premise: the 99 names of Allah taking mortal form—and the plaintiff argued that that in itself wasn't just disrespectful, it was downright blasphemous.

In defending himself before a Sharia court, Naif pointed out that when he was setting up the show's finances, his bank had a Sharia law adviser whose job it was to make sure everything the bank financed was compliant with Sharia law. Naif assured the court that he'd made the necessary adjustments and had gotten the advisor's approval for *THE 99*.

The court eventually decided in Naif's favor, but there was no way it or anyone else could have adjudicated the death threats that were then coming to Naif from some ISIS fighters, who had the same complaint as the man in Kuwait, but were far more inclined to use extra-judicial measures to make sure Naif wouldn't offend them again.

ISIS would never come close to making good on its threats; in just a few years, it would shrivel up and become a mere shadow of itself. Meanwhile, Naif went back to his original profession, psychology, and set to work expanding his practice. No such luck for The Hub, though: it folded just four years after its birth.

And what of the *New York Post*'s Andrea Peyser? In 2017, she announced that she'd be reducing her workload because of the multiple sclerosis that had been worsening ever since she'd been diagnosed with it in 2008.

Wikipedia describes multiple sclerosis as a disease of the brain and spinal cord and lists over two dozen possible symptoms including "cognitive problems" and "limited critical thinking." Wikipedia also says the cause of MS is "unknown," though readers familiar with the concept of karma might think they know why this misery was inflicted upon Ms. Peyser.

A few years ago, soon after The Hub folded, a friend and I had dinner with Margaret Loesch. All she had was a bowl of soup, but when the bill came, she reached for her purse. I slapped down my credit card first, telling her that she'd gotten screwed out of half a million dollars because of me. That bowl of soup was the least I could do.

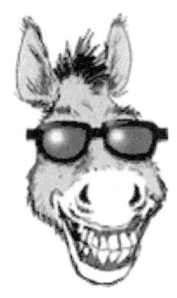

CHAPTER TEN
SAYING SOMETHING

I was in the West Hollywood office of a small theater chain, waiting outside its screening room as a low-level employee sat inside by himself, watching a five-minute student film I'd just written and directed. I really needed the chain to distribute it, but I wasn't particularly nervous about this guy's reaction. It had already been well-received by my fellow film students at UCLA, so I wasn't at all surprised when he stepped out of the screening room with a big smile and said, "It's funny all right…" but then he added, "…but I'd hate to suggest our customers are a bunch of asses."

Time seemed to stop as I tried to craft a response. The problem was, he was right about what that little film was saying. And it was part of a pattern with me.

If you give an adolescent boy a movie camera, chances are he'll make something inspired by his favorite TV shows, movies, video games or comic books. Something violent, probably, with lots of monsters, guns, fake blood and pratfalls. Juvenile stuff without much value, except as a time capsule to be pulled out of the attic after a couple of decades. But if you give a camera to that kid just a few years later, say around age 18, chances are he'll try to Say Something.

It's hard to explain exactly what Saying Something means. One producer I knew occasionally referred to the 'emesse' of a story (Hebrew for 'truth'). Another had a rule that none of his super-hero characters could defeat a villain just because they were better fighters; there had to be some other character-related reason for the hero's victory -- or defeat. Both these producers wanted there to be more to a story than simple action; they wanted substance, whether it was in the form of social criticism, characters forced to make life-altering decisions, or even satire. They rejected mindless action, and, by age 18, so had I.

My early 8mm silent films reflected the movies and TV shows I'd been watching, as well as particularly gory incidents I'd heard about in my history classes. Special effects, such as they were, came by way of colored filters, stop-motion manipulation of toys, and physical pin holes punched into the film to simulate gunfire. Then came high school, a time to get serious about the future, so I put away childish things, but only for a while. The trouble was, no future other than film and TV seemed interesting to me, so after being at UCLA for a while, I started making 8mm movies again. But now I wanted to Say Something. And what I needed to say was inspired by America's first mass school shooting.

In August of 1966, Charles Whitman, a 25-year-old student at the Austin campus of the University of Texas, stabbed his wife and his mother to death, then went to the top of the campus's tall bell tower with a rifle and began picking off the people below. Sixteen died before the police were able to kill Whitman. Unanswered was the question of why Whitman did it.

He'd written a long note for the authorities in which he said he didn't know his motivation, but he did know that one way or another he would be dead soon, and he requested that an autopsy be performed to see if there was an organic cause for his behavior. The doctors did find a brain tumor, but no one has ever been able to prove that the tumor caused him to kill all those people. Some have blamed the killings on the drugs Whitman was taking for his headaches, while others blamed his relationship with his domineering father. One doctor even claimed that the root cause was Whitman not having had enough playtime as a child.

Starting UCLA just two months after the Austin shootings, I would eventually develop my own theory. Like the Austin campus, UCLA was (and is) a huge place with an enormous student population (30,000 back then).

But for all the supposed crowding, it can also be lonely and isolating, especially for the many students who don't live on campus and commute from home. Classes take place in giant lecture halls, friends from high school aren't around anymore, and it's hard to make new friends when the lectures don't allow for much student–to–student interaction. So, my guess as to what might motivate a killer like Whitman was the pain of anonymity. I thought he might have been reacting violently to the indifference he felt all around him.

After the JFK assassination three years earlier, there'd been speculation that Oswald, an isolated loner, had been motivated by a need to feel noticed, even if it meant earning a particularly horrendous brand of notoriety. Ditto for Sirhan Sirhan, RFK's assassin, another frustrated, anonymous loner. (In 1976, *Taxi Driver* expanded on this theme by offering a story about an unstable loner who plotted an assassination in order to be noticed by a girl—which in turn inspired a real-life unstable loner to attempt an assassination in order to impress Jodi Foster, who acted in *Taxi Driver*).

BEYOND THE BAT

My planned film was eight years ahead of *Taxi Driver*, and I didn't quite have its budget. I did, however, have a take on the subject matter that I thought was unique. For me, ideas for stories often come from mixing two seemingly separate themes; I was already interested in the idea of anonymity as a motivation for a campus killer, but I didn't want to merely make a docu-drama about a disturbed person who hurts a lot of people. I wanted to do something with *attitude*, and maybe some irony.

And that led me to something I'd just read in my humanities class, Homer's *Odyssey*. In one of its most memorable episodes, Odysseus and some of his men are captured by a giant man-eating Cyclops. Trapped in this monster's cave, Odysseus is asked by the Cyclops for his name. Shrewdly, Odysseus gives him a name that sounds a lot like the Greek word for "nobody."

"Thanks, Nobody," the Cyclops glibly replies. "For that courtesy, I will eat you last."

Odysseus proceeds to get the Cyclops drunk, and once it falls into a stupor, he pokes its eye out. The creature wails loudly enough to wake up the other Cyclopes, all asleep in caves of their own. They shout into this one's cave: "Did someone hurt you? Did someone trick you?"

"Nobody hurt me! Nobody tricked me!" the blinded Cyclops shouts back from the bowels of his cave... So the other Cyclopes shrug and go back to sleep... and Odysseus is soon able to sneak away. Thus, crafty Odysseus proved that anonymity—being a nobody—isn't always a bad thing. Sometimes, it can even save your life.

In my little film, which was titled *Nobody* up front, lest anyone miss the point, we first see black-and-white images of a pale, nondescript protagonist wandering around a vast college campus, always alone, disconnected, ignored, unwanted.

Then, suddenly, we are at his home, in the bathroom. His hands are bloody, as is the hatchet he holds. He stares into the mirror as if asking himself, "Now what?"

He goes into a bedroom, takes a pistol from a nightstand, then steps over the blood-soaked bodies of his family as he exits his home. Soon, the house is a crime scene. Bodies are being taken out on stretchers, and a young detective is questioning a neighbor lady (silently, because I didn't have a camera with sound capability. But you get the idea, because you've seen interrogations like this a million times on the news: "He was always so quiet, I never would have guessed," etc., etc.)

In this story, the neighbor has paid so little attention to the killer next door, she can't even give the cop an approximation of how tall he was. But then the detective gets a break: a second detective comes out of the house with a driver's license he's found, and it's got a picture of the killer on it.

One of the detectives quickly finds the killer's car, which is parked near a bus station. The detective walks over to the station, and we see that the killer is indeed there, waiting to catch a Greyhound. Spotting the detective before the detective notices him, the killer reaches into his coat pocket and puts his hand on the butt of his pistol. Then, in quick succession, a bus pulls in, the detective goes over and stands by the bus's door to watch the passengers board... and fails to notice the killer as he passes right under his nose and gets onto the bus. The bus then pulls away from the station, and there's a fade to black.

Not a lot of people saw this thing, and only one person who did laughed at what I thought was a comedy, though a very dark, bleak one. Someone who'd been anonymous and ignored by the world had finally exploded because of it, but instead of facing the consequences, he was able to get away because of that very anonymity.

As for the cop, I saw him as a stand-in for society in general, which seemed (and still seems) all too eager to turn a blind eye to seriously troubled people. It might make you wonder if a society that is so intent on ignoring potentially dangerous people is also ignoring those who have the potential to do great things.

Nobody was not a class project. I wasn't even a film major when I shot it. I was just an undergraduate making home movies on campus, but I had already taken some film classes, the teachers had been encouraging, and I enjoyed making *Nobody* enough to finally see if I'd be let into the film school. Had I made that decision just a few months later, I might not have gotten into UCLA's film school—that's how popular the major was quickly becoming.

But as it stood, I didn't have to show anyone my film or any of the film criticism I'd written for my classes; I just checked a box and I was in. And that meant I would soon have to do another short film, something the film school called a Project One. But what would I want to say this time?

I'd signed up to be a film major in the spring of 1969, which meant that I would start work on my Project One in the fall. There was a lot going on back then, most notably the Vietnam war. But there was also the first moon landing, Woodstock, the Manson murders and a growing interest in environmentalism that would lead to the first Earth Day just a year later.

I was lying in bed on the night of the moon landing, thinking about one particular aspect of it: the astronauts had landed on the lunar surface in a vehicle called a Lunar Excursion Module (LEM). When they blasted off from the moon to return to their orbiting mothership, the plan was for them to leave part of the LEM behind on the surface of the moon. That fact aroused the budding environmentalist in me.

BEYOND THE BAT

"Everywhere we humans go, even the moon, we leave our garbage behind," I thought, and just like that, by combining two disparate concepts, I had an idea for my Project One. (Only one other student would have anything to say about the environment that year, and his film turned out to be a hectoring documentary about pollution.)

I called my Project One *Comforts of Home*, and it begins with a clean-cut young man with a suitcase entering a room of what might be a boarding house. Stepping into the room's bathroom, the expressionless young man takes a can of used, black motor oil from his suitcase and pours the stuff right into the bathtub. Then, as lilting xylophone music begins to play on the soundtrack, he drags a trashcan into his new bedroom and sets fire to its contents, so that a thick haze soon fills the room. Then he dumps garbage onto the carpet. Finally, he pulls a cassette player out of his suitcase and turns it on, and the soundtrack switches to traffic noise and the roar of airplane engines. At last, the young man feels comfortable, and as he stretches out in his easy chair, a satisfied smile creeps across his face.

Was he a symbol of mankind, hellbent on destroying its environment, or was he just a deranged individual who couldn't be comfortable until the inside of his new home looked, smelled and sounded like the world outside? Both, I felt, so I was pretty happy with this little statement of mine. But what would my teachers and fellow students think?

At the end of every quarter, the film school held days-long screenings of the finished films, and it wasn't just for fun; the aspiring filmmakers were being graded by their professors, and our grades would determine if we would be allowed to make another film. And if that wasn't enough pressure, after our films ran, we'd have to go to the front of the big theater and take questions and criticism from our teachers and fellow students.

I'll cut to the chase here, because my ultimate fate wasn't as dramatic as something else that went on during the screenings. *Comforts of Home* only got one comment, a technical one about the soundtrack; a few weeks later, I found out I'd passed. I was relieved, of course, but what made a more lasting impression on me was the nature of the comments the teachers made throughout the screenings.

If you were one of the students, there'd be no way you wouldn't have been afraid those teachers would tear your work to pieces right in front of you. And since the teachers were holding your future in their hands, they would be almost like gods to you, and not the kind, loving one from the New Testament. They would have seemed more like the angry, often-arbitrary one from the Old Testament.

But that wasn't the dynamic I observed at the screenings. Instead of being overly critical, the teachers were way too generous. An incoherent mess of a film would be called "poetic," while self-indulgent navel-gazing might be labeled "incisive." The teachers were obviously trying to be encouraging, but they were so eager to heap praise on stuff that was clearly garbage, they stopped being gods and became asses instead.

And just like that, I had half an idea for my next short film.

The other half was inspired by a cartoon in *Playboy* magazine. It showed a bunch of guys sitting in front of a fold-up screen on which a nature film called *Alonzo, Wild Stag of the North* was being projected. One of the guys is saying to another, "When you said you were going to show us a stag film, this wasn't what I had in mind." Ha ha.

Blending these two disparate inspirations, I came up with an idea for a film within a film. The inner film would be a stag film. A real one, or rather, one that looked like it was going to be real, and definitely not for the faint of heart. It would feature bestiality: a girl and a donkey.

The framing film would be in lush color; we'd be looking at a bed sheet tacked to a rustic-looking wall. The lights would go down, we would hear the whir of a projector, and up on the sheet, in grainy, scratchy black-and-white, we would see a girl brushing a donkey. She would somehow get aroused by doing this, so she would undress, and just when it looked like genital-to-genital contact was about ten seconds away, the camera would pull back from the sheet on the wall to reveal that the audience for this thing is made up entirely of donkeys. Only they wouldn't be actual donkeys; they would be actors wearing donkey heads, much like the character of Bottom in *A Midsummer Night's Dream*. And the donkey heads would be given very specific facial hair, glasses and other markings so they would be instantly recognizable as donkey versions of our more asinine film professors.

I shared this idea with three friends from my Project One class, and they liked it—a lot—but they had two reservations. First, they believed the donkeys shouldn't be made up to look like our teachers, because it would make the film too much of an inside joke. (A year later, a student named Randy Cook used toy soldiers and stop-motion animation to ridicule one of our teachers -- by name. I don't know what grade Randy got for that, but he went on to earn three Oscars for his visual effects on the *Lord of the Rings* movies.)

The other issue my three friends had with my new idea pertained to the potential use of grainy black-and-white film. They didn't think the film-within-the-film should look like that. We were film students, after all, learning how to make film look good; why not display what we'd learned?

BEYOND THE BAT

Notice that the first-person plural crept into the previous paragraph. My three friends wanted to make this film with me, and each of us would eventually chip in a quarter of the budget. We'd each have an assigned task, too; I would be the writer/director, another of us would be the cinematographer, another would produce, and the fourth would be our crewman, setting up the lights and running the generator. And, as per another of their suggestions, our donkeys would be real.

An afternoon at a nude modeling agency on Hollywood Boulevard netted us a model named Jeanette. She got a hundred dollars for her day's work in a barn in the northern San Fernando Valley. A few days after shooting Jeanette's scenes, the four of us drove even farther north into the Valley to shoot the film's framing sequence at the notorious Spahn Movie Ranch, where our producer had rented us a stable full of donkeys. And yes, the Spahn Ranch was notorious *before* we shot there. Manson and some of his followers had been busted months earlier, leaving only the scary remnants of his family at the ranch. I wanted to know why our producer had chosen to schedule a night shoot there. "Didn't you read about those people in the paper? They have orgies there," he told me, somehow managing not to actually drool at the prospect.

As our night of shooting at the Spahn Ranch was ending, there was no sign of an orgy, but one of the family members, a kid with a straw cowboy hat and a big knife on his belt, sidled over to our producer and asked him for a little extra money, because Charlie and the others were having to pay lots of legal fees. Our producer brusquely told the kid that we had already paid the agreed-upon fee, and that was the end of it, as far as he was concerned. Downcast, the kid walked off into the dark night, and we got the hell out of there as fast as we could. The sense of menace surrounding that place was presented with dead-on accuracy in Tarantino's *Once Upon a Time in Hollywood*.

Our little film, which I called *Ass*, came together quickly after that. We were able to use UCLA's sound mixing room to create our simple soundtrack (the whir of a projector, and at the end, the sound of several donkeys braying appreciatively). Then, on a night when student films were being informally screened in our big theater, we slipped in *Ass*, even though it had been made entirely outside the jurisdiction of the film school, and without any faculty advisor.

Later that night, I couldn't sleep—that's how excited I was about the look of the film, something I had virtually nothing to do with. My partners had been right about making the film-within-a-film look as good as we could, and up on that huge screen, its vibrant color and flawless lighting looked as good to me as almost any feature I'd seen there. I should have felt nothing more than relief and slept soundly, but that night, it seemed like professionalism was at last a real possibility—make that a likelihood—and I had somehow caught a glimpse of a glittering future.

Money was a consideration, too. At that time there were only a couple of commercial outlets for student films; small companies—just a person or two—who would assemble compilations of student films and exhibit them on college campuses or in art theaters. They didn't pay much, but at least we would get back the money we'd put in—if they wanted *Ass* in their compilations, and I was pretty sure they would.

Because *Ass* had an attractive naked woman in it, I figured there might be a secondary market for it: adult theaters. I hoped they'd want to run *Ass* as a short subject to go with their feature-length fare, which is why I was at the office of that small chain of X-rated theaters, where the lowest ranking employee got the point of *Ass* all too clearly. After just a brief moment to compose some bullshit, I assured him that the film's only statement was the simple role reversal of having donkeys in the audience.

The guy gave me a skeptical look, then said, "Let's see what my boss thinks." So once again, I waited outside the screening room for five minutes, until his boss came out, also with a big smile. But this man said nothing about the film suggesting anyone was an ass. All he said was, he needed *his* boss to take a look at it.

The big boss was the owner of the theater chain, a tall blond man in his mid-thirties named Shan Sayles. He too came out of the screening room smiling, and also without saying anything about suggesting anyone was an ass. Instead, he offered to buy a print of the film.

I left Sayles's office with a small check, but it was enough to reimburse us for about a quarter of our budget. And there was something else I left with, too: the realization that the lowest person on the totem pole could sometimes be the most perceptive.

Now that I had some money in the bank again, I could get back to my schoolwork, which consisted mainly of a Project Two short film. But what was I going to say this time?

I'd been watching a lot of old movies on my tiny black-and-white TV. Not so much to learn about story structure or dialogue, but rather, to study their directorial techniques. I noticed that a lot of directors resisted visual stasis whenever they could. These were "moving pictures" after all, and even when characters were sitting talking to each other, some directors treated their cameras as if they were living eyes, constantly moving around, focusing and refocusing, never still. I liked that.

Another thing I liked back then was an album by the English group The Nice, called *Ars Longa Vita Brevis*. The leader of the group was Keith Emerson, who would later form Emerson, Lake and Palmer. As much as I enjoyed The Nice's music, it was the album's title that really intrigued me. It's Latin for "art endures, life is short," which certainly holds true for the great artists, whose work lives on far beyond their lifetimes. It's not so true for the lesser ones though, like the elderly actors who sit at sparsely attended autograph tables at comic conventions, their TV shows and movies long forgotten by all but their most dedicated fans. Yet there they are, their aged flesh having long outlived their artistry.

Combining these two things—the durability of (some) art and directorial technique—I was came up with a story for my Project Two. It would be about a young writer who blames his lack of success on the fact that he hasn't experienced much of life and thus, cannot write authoritatively about anything. So he's considering killing himself. He writes a suicide note, paces back and forth in his apartment with a pistol to his head, but ultimately, he can't do it. Instead, he goes off to experience life, and gets more than he bargained for: he's picked up hitchhiking by a couple who are on the run from the law, and he's almost killed when the cops catch up to them. The end.

Except there was a big twist: during the scene when the writer is pacing back and forth, pistol to his head, the gun accidentally goes off, appearing to kill the actor who is portraying the writer. But the film goes along on its merry way, continuing to pan back and forth as if the actor were still pacing. Then the camera goes outside, where it pans down some stairs, as if following someone who can't be seen. Soon, a car stops to pick up someone who can only be seen by the car's occupants. They speak to him and respond as if he is answering them, though all we hear is silence from an empty passenger seat.

Once this idea is established, the other actors disappear one by one until all we're left with are shots of blank walls and some furious camera motion during a fight scene from which the actors have been subtracted. The title I chose for this, of course, was "Ars Longa Vita Brevis."

When we stood in front of the screen after our films ran, we usually waited for someone from the audience to say something before we spoke. Had I done that, I'm pretty sure the first, and possibly only response would have been something like, "what the fuck *was* that?"

And I probably would've responded in kind. But I couldn't afford to do that just then, because I had very recently been admitted to the University's grad school for screenwriting, and only by the skin of my teeth, I'd been told. So, the last thing I wanted to do was make those kinds of waves just then. Thus, as a defensive move, I decided to speak first. I told the audience that the film they'd just seen was an experiment, and I wanted very much to hear everyone's interpretation of it.

It turned out to be the right thing to say. I got all kinds of responses, most of them off-the-wall, some clearly influenced by recreational drugs, but none that expressed the hostility the film probably deserved. Afterward, I even got a kind word from the acting/directing teacher who'd spent ten endless weeks berating me earlier in the year. She told me that, having seen how I handled actors on film, she felt she had gotten through to me after all, and was now willing to bump up the grade she'd given me.

I politely declined; her grade no longer mattered, because I had already gotten into grad school, and besides, the real lessons I learned about directing and acting were things I picked up that very day: first, always try to take control of a situation; second, when you ask for somebody's opinion, it makes them feel important and therefore more inclined to look at you favorably; and finally, when they do offer their opinion, act like it matters to you.

There you have it: four short films, a body of work that turned man's indifference to his fellow man into a black comedy; that viewed the poisoning of our environment as a symptom of species-wide insanity; that looked at its own audience and called them asses; and that said our artistic endeavors are far more important than our miserable, trivial lives. Misanthropy and nihilism in full bloom before I was old enough to buy a drink. And, it turned out to be the last time in a very long career that I would be able to express those sentiments exactly the way I wanted to: uncensored and with no notes from anyone.

You might wonder who in the world would have wanted to hire someone like that to make a movie, but there was one such person: Shan Sayles, owner of that adult theater chain in West Hollywood. After *Ass* had been running in his theaters for a while, he invited the four of us to his office. He had an offer: he would pay us to make a full-length feature for him!

If I'd had a crystal ball at that moment, it would've told me that Mr. Sayles's offer wasn't quite as generous as it sounded. Like others in that business, Sayles knew exactly how much one of his low budget features would cost to make, and the amount he intended to give us would barely be enough to make that feature—cheaply—and with only enough left over for us to pay our rents and put food on our tables until we started on the next film for him. And it would go on and on like that.

The crystal ball would have also told me that we wouldn't be able to use those films as calling cards to get other work, because no matter how handsomely produced they were, or how witty the dialogue was, we wouldn't have been able to put our names on the films. That was because back then, those films occupied a gray legal area.

Filmmakers and theater owners were constantly being busted for obscenity, and a big part of their operating expenses were fees paid to First

Amendment lawyers. And, had I been reckless enough to put my name on the film(s) anyway, not only would I have run the risk of legal trouble, I would have also been very likely to find myself stuck forever in the sexploitation/porn ghetto, never taken seriously enough to work on mainstream movies or television.

If that crystal ball had been really, really prescient, it would have also told me that the business to which I was being offered entry would change quite a bit over the length of my potential career. Within just a year or two, the legal problems would fade away as hardcore porn became more or less legal, but only a few years after that, many of the adult theaters would close because people were buying video recorders that allowed them to watch films at home. And with recorders in so many homes, producers would begin making stuff on videotape which was much cheaper-looking than film. So much for our vaunted production values!

Soon enough, the folks at home would start copying their videos and giving them away, which is technically piracy, but the laws against it were next to impossible to enforce, especially as they pertained to the adult film business, owing to law enforcement's rocky history with that industry.

And finally, the crystal ball also would have told me that by the early 2000s, when I'd be in my early 50s and theoretically at the top of my game as a writer/director, there would be a thing called the Internet, which would be only too happy to give away my carefully crafted erotica—for free.

But even if I had known what the future held, I still would have been tempted by what Mr. Sayles was offering; I needed rent money, I would've loved to Say Something in an erotic vein, and I would have been happy to move into a social circle that would include actresses who might have made up for that orgy we missed at the Spahn Ranch — and then Sayles added, "It'll be a gay film. You guys don't have a problem with that, do you?"

Cue needle scratch.

For the other guys, that was an easy question. Their interests—cinematography, line producing and general crew work—had no relevance to the content of the films they hoped to make. Experience would be experience, a currency accepted almost anywhere. Sure, their names wouldn't be on the films, but word would get around that they knew what they were doing in their respective crafts, and for them, one job would lead to another.

Not for me, though. I had no knowledge of the world Sayles wanted me to write for, and no affinity for it. To put it a different way, I had nothing to say, and as the writer/director of the group, I would be expected to take the creative lead. A year earlier, I'd interviewed Russ Meyer, who made a fortune directing low budget sexploitation films, all very clearly based on his own fantasies and fetishes—which happened to strike a chord with what was then called "the raincoat crowd"—men who went by themselves to see movies that featured naked women. Russ made the best of those movies, and they were that good because he was making the kind of movies that he found arousing. If I accepted Sayles' offer, I wouldn't be doing that. For starters, someone else would have to write the script; what did I know about gay sex? Then there would be casting; how would I—or any of the four of us, for that matter—be able to tell which actors were the type of guy who would physically appeal to other guys? Tall and muscular? Thin and androgynous? Big and hairy? And that would just be the beginning of a series of challenges I'd face if I took the job. But by far the worst part of it would be that the intended audience would know instantly and with complete certainty how compromised I was. And it just wouldn't have been fair to them.

What I'm getting at here is the line between amateurism and professionalism. Professional writer/directors figure out ways to do at least a creditable job with whatever material they're hired to do, and I would not be a professional in that sense for at least another decade.

What was perhaps a more professional attitude was articulated by Jim, our all-around crewman: "Fucking is fucking," he said, and that sentiment allowed him and my other two partners to take Sayles up on his invitation to go see one of his films and decide if they'd like to make one themselves. Ultimately, they didn't accept Sayles's offer. Tom, our cinematographer, ended up teaching cinematography, while Jim and our line producer, Mike, never made it into the business. I didn't go with them to Sayles's movie; saying something is important, but it's just as important as knowing when you have nothing to say.

THE END... Except for:

Weird Coda #1: Clark Dugger, the gifted student-actor who so convincingly pretended to accidentally shoot himself onscreen in *Ars Longa Vita Brevis*, came through our filming without a scratch. He's now a photographer living in Palm Springs. Not so fortunate was another actor who worked on a show I wrote for. That was Jon-Erik Hexum, and the show was called *Cover Up*.

He was on the set in October of 1984, waiting around between takes, when he idly put a pistol to his temple and pulled the trigger. He knew the gun had a blank in it, but he didn't know that the impact of a blank at very close range can be as lethal as a bullet, and in his case, it was.

During the show's ensuing hiatus, Hexum's character was replaced, as was some of the writing staff. A new supervising producer/head writer stepped in, and he'd liked a sample script I'd written the previous year. So, with the *Mike Hammer* show coming to an untimely end, I called this producer to see if he'd take a chance on me writing a script for his show. And he did.

The script went smoothly and quickly, too, because a Writers' Guild strike was looming. The show's staff writers and story editors had little time to rewrite me, and when the episode aired in the spring of 1985, it played pretty much the way I wrote it. It was my first produced TV script, and I don't think I would have had the opportunity to write it, had it not been for that horrible accident which mirrored the one in my student film.

Weird Coda #2: In 2016, Keith Emerson, whose choice of an album title inspired me so many years earlier, committed suicide by shooting himself in the head. And no, there was no way he could have seen the little movie I named after his album… which I still listen to every now and then. *Ars* is indeed *longa*!

STAN BERKOWITZ

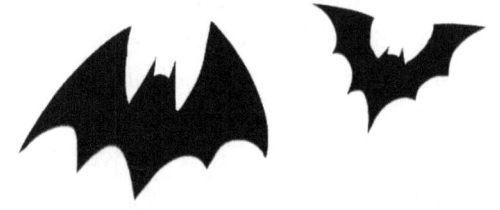

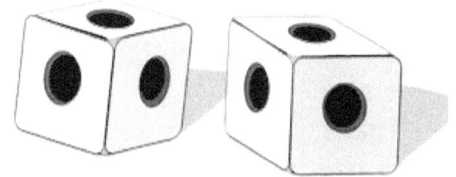

CHAPTER ELEVEN
PLAYING THE ODDS

Years ago, a novelist friend told me about one of the biggest problems she faced while trying to make a living in a very competitive field: "You have to put everything into learning to do what you really want to do, and if it doesn't work out, you're not prepared to do anything else. There's no fallback position."

She was saying this from behind a department store counter where she was selling purses... on the same day her second novel was published.

Since my teens, I'd wanted to be involved in making movies, but growing up in Southern California and constantly hearing how hard it was to get into the business, I knew enough not to make that novelist's mistake: I had a Plan B in place by the beginning of my sophomore year of college. It was to be a critic or journalist, and that eventually led me to a part-time job editing my college newspaper's entertainment section.

That's where I met Lucky—not his real name, but not a bad description of him back then. Tall and easygoing, he'd done his undergraduate work in the Midwest and had made a well-regarded student film there. He'd also been a musician, a nationally-ranked athlete and, more important as far as I was concerned, he had experience writing movie reviews for his small hometown's newspaper.

Like me, he was about to start UCLA's master's program in screenwriting, and also like me, he saw a future at the *Daily Bruin*. (I figured he had a Plan B, too.) His movie review samples were solid, his taste was mainstream but with an appreciation of the avant-garde, and his negative reviews weren't malicious. So I asked him to start writing reviews for the paper, and we quickly became friends. By the end of grad school, we were working on a spec script together.

Lucky was personable and made friends easily, qualities I didn't have (and, many might say, still don't), and I figured that no matter how much work—or how little—he put into our script, it wouldn't matter; it would be his congenial personality that would get the script sold. Producers who read it would want to work with him (and they'd be stuck with me in the bargain.)

Lucky's personality didn't turn out to be enough. Or maybe our script wasn't good enough. Whatever the reason, all we got were a few nibbles, a cheap option or two from would-be producers, and then nothing. To support myself, I went off to work on the crew of a low-budget film, while Lucky was lucky enough to step into a job in publicity at a record company.

In the mid-1970s, the music business was rolling in cash. Record companies' publicity departments could easily afford to hire young people who were wired into the culture, even if some of them really wanted to be doing something else, like making music—or writing film scripts. So Lucky was a good fit.

But the record companies were also notoriously unstable, and after only months, there was a personnel shift that left Lucky briefly unemployed. Luck was with him again, though, and he was almost immediately snapped up by a prestigious public relations firm that handled old-school entertainers as well as headline rock and pop performers. He was given an office in the back where he wrote press releases—and spec scripts. He made no secret of this extracurricular writing; he even spent years trying to convince one of the agency's partners to produce a script he wrote.

One of the reasons the agency might not have been too bothered by Lucky's extracurricular work was that the agency's older guys, like the record company execs, probably figured it was worth it to have someone in the office who was a lot more familiar with the youth zeitgeist than they were. Another reason they tolerated Lucky's scriptwriting was that Lucky didn't cost them very much. And he never pushed hard for more, because he figured he'd be out of there soon enough, with a script of his in production.

Skipping today's dessert in exchange for pie in the sky didn't go over well at his home. Since grad school, Lucky had been married to a girl from his hometown, a freelancer who did a little photography, a little writing and little publicity work. As time passed and they entered their early thirties, she got tired of living like a grad student, especially in affluent West Los Angeles, among friends and neighbors who were starting serious careers in show business.

"Shouldn't [Lucky] join the Publicists' Guild?" she finally asked me one day.

They had obviously been arguing about it, and I figured Lucky's position was that if he joined that Guild he might've gotten better pay, but he would have had to work a lot harder. And that meant he'd no longer have time for his spec scripts.

Being in a similar position myself (but without a wife to advise me), I told Lucky's wife that I thought Lucky would undoubtedly be a very good full-time publicist—he had a perfect personality for it—but he wouldn't be happy. He'd have to make too many compromises hyping inferior acts, and worse, he'd no longer have time to write his spec scripts.

After explaining this to her, I didn't give it any more thought, but a few months later, she called early one morning to say she and Lucky were separating. The reason for the early call, she said, was that she wanted me (and, I assume their other friends) to hear it from her before we heard it from someone else. Looking back, I figure she must have been afraid that "someone else" would accuse her of being too money hungry or, perhaps, unfaithful. She didn't articulate any of that, though. She just said the split had been brewing a long time, and everything would ultimately work out for the best.

As it turned out, she really was looking for a new partner, one she hoped would furnish her with the lifestyle she'd been wanting for so long. But I didn't know that yet. From what little she told me back then, a reconciliation still sounded possible.

A day or two later, I had dinner with Lucky and saw a side of him I hadn't seen before: an astounding capacity for denial. When everything goes so well for you throughout your childhood and into your twenties, as it had for Lucky, you don't develop much in the way of coping skills. Thus, when things go wrong in adulthood, it's either someone else's fault or you just deny that anything's gone wrong. At our dinner, Lucky wasn't going to mention the separation to me, and when I finally pressed him on it, he told me he was fine, and no, he wasn't going to accuse her of infidelity or of searching for a new partner. There was just something wrong with her, that's all... as if she'd have to be crazy to leave a guy like him.

Oooooookaaaaay, I thought, as long as he's not too upset, and she isn't either, does it really matter if they have drastically different views of their new situation?

Six months later, Lucky was still living alone in the little apartment he'd once shared with his wife when he got another blow: his agency fired him. The business was changing, and they could no longer afford to have someone sitting in the back who wasn't fully committed to the company's mission.

So, what now? A woman Lucky and I knew had a part-time gig writing term papers for foreign kids going to college in the Los Angeles area, and she was leaving that to go work with her future husband at a business he was starting. Would Lucky like to have her contacts? Yes, he would. He'd had no other offers.

At the time, the term paper business operated in a gray area between the legal and the illegal. The authors of the papers claimed they were only writing "research papers" designed to impart information to students who would then write term papers that bore no resemblance whatsoever to the research papers. In practice, of course, the students turned in the research papers as if they were their own.

BEYOND THE BAT

The grad students and out-of-work writers who actually wrote the papers might ask what difference it made if students from Indonesia who came to Los Angeles for MBAs didn't remember F. Scott Fitzgerald once they got back to Indonesia. To me, though, the most compromising aspect of this work was the need to make sure the papers weren't too insightful or too well-written, because it would be obvious to the teachers that the students could not have written them.

So that was Lucky's constraint—not writing too well or too insightfully—when he became a one-man term paper mill around the time he turned thirty-five.

If you could say one thing for the term paper work, it was steady. It paid Lucky's bills, and that allowed him to continue writing spec scripts… and continue hoping his wife would come back. For the first years of their separation, she wouldn't pull the divorce trigger, so maybe she really wasn't sure about leaving him for good. Or maybe she just needed an easy way of keeping the wrong men from getting too close. Whatever the case, Lucky, a handsome, desirable guy, never stopped considering himself a married man and never touched another woman, even as his estranged wife was dating other men. Lucky's screenwriting efforts were equally unrewarding: a small nonunion assignment here, a few hundred dollars there.

So, after just a few years in the term paper business, Lucky stopped writing spec scripts. By age forty-six, he was a full-time term paper writer who wrote capsule book reviews on the side. And that's when a sudden massive heart attack killed him.

The doctor who cut Lucky open didn't find the expected clogged arteries, burst aorta or undiagnosed heart defect. Didn't find evidence of a drug overdose, either. Lucky's heart just stopped one morning, and he was dead before he hit the floor. The doctor called it an "electrical failure." They happen, but not very often.

Lucky kept a detailed journal, which included mentions of medications he was using. It noted allergy pills, and also, half a Valium at bedtime so he could get to sleep. He drank a little wine, occasionally smoked weed and had two cups of strong coffee in the morning to help him write those B minus-level college essays all day.

Taken as a whole, none of what he was using would've been enough to kill anyone, but Lucky had high blood pressure all his life—it had gotten him out of the draft—and some of his friends believed the combination of that and the allergy meds' antihistamines might've caused the electrical failure. (It was only a few years later that allergy and cold medication companies started giving warnings to people with high blood pressure.)

That explanation was good enough for me and most of his other friends, but his family didn't buy it. They were prominent in their small hometown, and when they looked at Lucky's life through their Midwestern lens, all they saw was an unattached middle-aged man with a small apartment and an old car—someone who was barely making a living doing something that might've been illegal. And, he had no obvious path to a better future. So they assumed he killed himself.

I wondered how long his family had seen him as a candidate for suicide. Did it occur to them only after he died, or had they been thinking that for years? If it was the latter, did Lucky know? If he did, would it have been just one more thing to put on his denial list? Whatever the case, the doctor who performed Lucky's autopsy wasn't the county coroner, but rather, a private doctor hired by the family, so discretion could be assured.

To me, the suicide theory was absurd. It would have been an admission of failure that Lucky never would have acknowledged. Besides, everyone knew he would've kept on writing term papers and hoping his wife would come back until he was at least a hundred, if his heart had let him.

The lingering question I have about Lucky's life is, what stopped him from having a career as a screenwriter? If you'd read just a few pages of any of his spec scripts, you might've thought he was a perfectly competent screenwriter. There'd be natural-sounding dialogue, appropriate visual grammar and all the rest. But if you'd read the whole thing, you might have been angered, as were so many of his friends. You might've found yourself asking if this writer understood or cared about concepts like theme, character development, metaphor and subtext—elements that help define fiction and give it weight and value.

When his writing teachers at film school took him to task for this, he'd shrug off their criticism; what did they know? When everything has come so easily to you during your formative years, shouldn't screenwriting be easy, too -- and not the often painful, soul-searching job it can be for so many? Instead of getting a sense of any of that in Lucky's scripts, you'd see a simplistic form of self-therapy. Typically, his stories involved someone of his own basic description who worked in a media-focused industry similar to the one in which Lucky had worked. This character would have a girlfriend who'd be tempted by the flashy lifestyle of a high-rolling promoter type, and she would soon leave our hero for this other guy. But then the promoter's foundations would be shown to be built on sand, and boy would get girl back. The end.

Except for the happy ending, this was transparently his own story. And it was this all-too-obvious wish fulfillment that infuriated those of us who read his scripts. Where was the insight? Where was character development? Had his characters learned anything from their experiences? Certainly not the leading man; he just kept his head low and followed his course, unable, or more likely, unwilling to change. His position in the script as the hero was attained purely because he lacked faults. He was just a decent guy who never bothered anyone and wasn't terribly ambitious. In most movies, this kind of character would be the boring fiancé of a leading lady who's about to meet a less stable though far more appealing love interest. But Lucky wouldn't have considered making the girl his main character. Or the promoter. The focus of the script had to be him, and more specifically, his presentation of himself as a stable, basically passive guy in a world of phonies.

Had he ever taken a hard-headed look at himself? Had he ever heard of metaphor or any of those other things good fiction needs? Of course he had; remember, he was also an occasional book reviewer, and for the *New York Times*, no less. But either he didn't care, or more likely, he couldn't see his own work as clearly as he could see others'. Most writers can't, which is why we need feedback. But when his friends tried to give feedback to him, we were met with a wall of resistance.

As he was handing me one of his scripts to read, Lucky confided that another friend had already read it and had been so harshly critical, Lucky decided he would never speak to him again. Then he added, "If you don't like this script, you don't like me." "So now I'm supposed to give you my honest opinion?" I asked. "Just be constructive," he said.

I tried, but later, in a two-hour phone call, I wasn't able to get past page five with him, for all the defensiveness I met. So I gave up. So did his other friends. And eventually, so did he. He was immersed in other people's fiction, yet as far as I could tell, he didn't understand the basic purpose of fiction, at least as it applied to his own efforts.

Certainly, there would have been no compelling reason to see a movie based on any of his scripts. But couldn't that be said about lots of movies that do get made? So, could it have possibly been nothing more than bad luck that stymied Lucky's screenwriting career?

Thousands of movie scripts are written every year, but only a few hundred movies are made. Lucky and the rest of us were well aware of these odds by the time we got to grad school. But for Lucky, 10- or 20-to-1 odds must not have seemed like such a long shot; all through school he'd placed somewhere between the 90th and 99th percentile in just about everything he'd tried, hadn't he? So how much luck would he need to hit a 10- or 20-to-1 shot?

More luck than he got. Chance can be funny that way; sometimes you make an easy bet on red, but black keeps coming up on the wheel, and then, out of the blue, lightning will strike you. What are the odds of that? For Lucky, that lightning bolt was the failure of his heart. The doctor pegged the odds of it at ten million to one.

A few weeks after Lucky died, two of his other friends and I were cleaning out his apartment, bagging his clothes for Goodwill. I found a couple of pairs of new dress socks that still had tags on them and decided to keep them. Three years later, I was wearing a pair when my colleagues and I from the *Batman/Superman* animated show were called onto the stage of the Century Plaza Hotel to accept Emmys. I thought about Lucky when I slipped off the socks that night, wondering how he would have felt seeing me up on that stage, accepting an Emmy. Would he have been jealous? If he'd've been, he probably would have denied it. Would he have written it all off to luck? Of that, I'm certain.

STAN BERKOWITZ

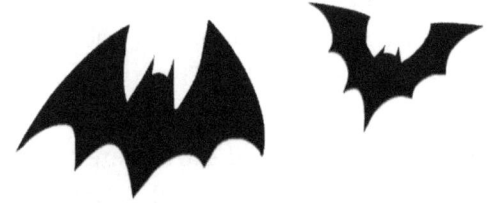

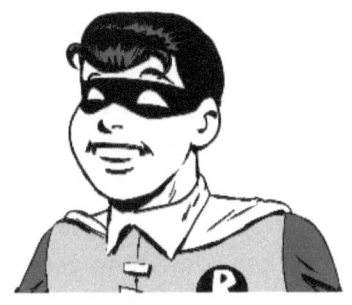

CHAPTER TWELVE
THE ROBIN PROBLEM

I was entering Southern California's Honda Center arena with an old friend when one of the venue's employees stopped us, asked to see our tickets, then told us she'd get us better seats. It was a curious offer. I'd bought general admission tickets so I could experience this arena show like any other member of the public... even though I'd helped write it. Now I was wondering if this woman could have possibly recognized me from my picture in the program. What else could it have been?

Once she led us into the main hall, I found out what it was. The place was practically empty, and this lady was trying to crowd everyone as close as she could to the stage. I assumed this was for the benefit of the performers' morale, but what about mine? I was now pretty sure my tiny share of the show's profits would turn out to be zilch, but what was far worse was the sudden overwhelming guilt I felt. I was ashamed I hadn't done more during the show's writing process to make sure this wouldn't happen.

When something goes wrong for you, it's natural to try to find someone else to blame. And if there doesn't happen to be anyone else, the next best thing is to pretend nothing went wrong.

Years earlier, when I was a freelance journalist, the *Los Angeles Times* sent me and that old friend of mine, David Lees, to the set of a movie called *Beyond the Poseidon Adventure* to do a story about it. Its producer/director, Irwin Allen, had earned the nickname "The Master of Disaster" for practically inventing the disaster film genre by producing *The Poseidon Adventure* and *The Towering Inferno*. More recently, he'd just finished directing another disaster movie, this one about killer bees and titled *The Swarm*.

Allen had also been the producer of some TV series I'd loved as a child: *Voyage to the Bottom of the Sea*, *The Time Tunnel* and *Lost in Space*, but at the Burbank Studios that afternoon, David and I were at a bit of a loss for things to talk to him about.

The movie he was making seemed like an unnecessary sequel to a movie that hadn't seemed all that necessary itself, although this new one did boast future Oscar winners Sally Field and Michael Caine.

Unfortunately, neither was on the set that day, and the best I could do was start my questions for Allen with some career stuff, trying to work backward from his most recent feature.

But as soon as the words *The Swarm* left my mouth, Allen's manner abruptly changed. Before, he'd reminded me a bit of my family doctor: smarter than you, but willing to explain things in a fatherly way. A mention of the killer bees, though, sent Allen hurrying back to the set.

A few minutes later, his visibly embarrassed publicist came over to us and said there would be no interview, and it had to do with the mention of *The Swarm*, which was a box office failure. "Babe Ruth hit a lot of homeruns," the publicist said, "but he struck out sometimes, too."

To a freelancer, not getting an interview means not getting paid, so being asked to leave the set was bad news. Also bad news, but this time, not for us: when the editor of the *Times*' entertainment section heard what happened, he printed a small item about it, clearly intended to—dare I say it?—sting Mr. Allen.

Beyond the Poseidon Adventure was released to negative reviews and low attendance. Irwin Allen, who was then in his mid-sixties, would continue on as a producer for a few more years, but he would never direct another movie. His attempt to forget about *The Swarm* only led to the wound being reopened.

For me, that arena show, *Batman Live*, will always be a bit of a wound, though it was generally forgotten almost as soon as it came out. It wasn't bad, it was just something that wasn't suited to its own medium.

Arena shows are unique; the best of them, like the *Mamma Mia* show, feature sing-along music, while others offer things that you can't otherwise see in a live venue, like *Walking with Dinosaurs'* gigantic mechanical creatures. Lesser arena events, like the one that featured Marvel's superheroes, are glorified stunt shows highlighted by elaborately choreographed fights and motorcycle stunts.

When Alan Burnett and I went to New York to meet with several DC Comics executives and the show's English producer, Nick Grace, we were looking at a blank page. There was no idea at all of what the story for the show would be, but at that point my interest was less in the story than in what would fill the floor of the arena. Would it be the Batmobile and/or the Batcycle doing vehicular stunts? Elaborate fights? Or maybe there would be some kind of tribute to the work of the late comics artist Dick Sprang (his actual name!), who would often send Batman on after-hours adventures to lavish industrial exhibitions where he'd chase bad guys across the keys of giant typewriters, over-sized cash registers and the like. Or what about using Clayface, the gigantic blob-like creature whose story was told so well in *Batman: The Animated Series*?

All those suggestions were met with only slightly varying degrees of disinterest. Clayface's nixing was especially pronounced; Nick Grace didn't want any "unrealistic" characters in the show, so the question of what would then fill the arena floor was answered pretty quickly: it would be chairs — for the audience. One end of the arena would be blocked off, a stage would be built there, and the rest of the arena would be set up pretty much like a theater. The only concession to the vastness of the venues would be that the stage wouldn't be in the standard proscenium shape; instead, it would jut outward into the audience in a V-shape, and the house's most expensive seats would be along the legs of that V.

With all that determined, we started talking about story, and I suggested the show start with a young boy suffering a terrible trauma. At first, the audience would assume this is young Bruce Wayne, but as we'd get deeper into this opening sequence, the details would stop matching up, and we would soon realize this kid isn't Bruce Wayne, but rather, the future Joker.

This idea didn't even make it past our lunch break. The Joker would still be our villain, of course, but it was quickly decided that the boy would be the young Bruce Wayne, and we would then proceed to do the Batman/Robin origin story... which brought up — for me, at least—something I'll call "The Robin Problem."

With the rise of the Dark Knight/angry vigilante version of Batman, it's sometimes forgotten that he was originally designed to be a master detective, somewhat in the mold of Sherlock Holmes. Robin, who didn't show up in the comics until the year after Batman premiered in 1939, was intended to be a character younger readers could identify with, and also serve as a Watson to Batman's Holmes. Without Robin, or someone like him, all of Batman's deductive logic would have to be explained in his own thought bubbles.

These were the reasons the early Batman writers had for creating the character of Robin, but what was *Batman's* reason for making Robin his crime fighting partner? Sure, the kid was a gifted acrobat, but he was still a preadolescent, and taking someone that young on dangerous vigilante missions was, and is, tantamount to child endangerment.

Batman's thinking back in 1940 was that Dick Grayson had just seen his parents murdered (like the young Bruce Wayne had) and was now intent on going off on his own to seek revenge. It would be safer, Batman thought, to take the kid under his wing and solve the case together. So, Batman makes Dick swear an oath to support justice and fair play and gives him a room in Wayne Manor.

Thus begins a decades-long relationship that's always been fraught with innuendo. A wealthy bachelor taking a preadolescent boy as his ward?

Hmmm... The two of them cavorting all night in masks, capes and tights? Call the vice squad! Which is pretty much what a psychiatrist named Frederic Wertham tried to do in his 1954 book, *Seduction of the Innocent*, a wide-ranging attack on comic books. Batman and Robin, or if you prefer, Bruce and Dick, survived that storm, but when executives at ABC TV decided to do a campy *Batman* TV series in 1966, they felt compelled to welcome an elderly "Aunt Harriet" to stately Wayne Manor so there would be a sort of chaperone to, umm, separate the boys from the men.

When Batman was entrusted to directors Tim Burton, Christopher Nolan and Zack Snyder, they left Robin out of their films. Most of us who wrote for the animated series would have preferred to leave out Robin, too, but we were stuck with him for the same reasons the comics writers need him: so kids have someone to identify with and so Batman has someone to explain plot stuff to. Any retelling of the Robin origin story poses two big questions for its writers. First, why would Bruce Wayne take Dick Grayson into his home—didn't Gotham City have orphanages? Second, why would Bruce tell Dick he is Batman, and thus surrender his carefully guarded secret identity—to a child?

Once it was decided *Batman Live* would include Robin (for the same old reasons), Alan Burnett offered an elegant answer to the question of why Bruce Wayne would take young Dick Grayson into his home. Commissioner Gordon would be presented as an old friend of Bruce's, and, like everyone else in Gotham City, he knew that years earlier, Bruce's parents had been murdered.

Now, with a similar fate having befallen young Dick Grayson, who would be better suited than millionaire Bruce with all his resources to keep an eye on the boy while the police attempt to bring the murderers to justice? When Gordon put it that way to Bruce, there was no way Bruce could refuse, even if he'd wanted to.

The answer to the second question, the one about Bruce giving up his secret identity, wasn't nearly as elegant. We figured it would only be because of an accident or dire necessity that Bruce would share his secret with anyone. Accordingly, we had the Joker take over Wayne Manor for some reason and then briefly leave Bruce and Dick alone while both are tied to chairs. Bruce could easily break free, but doing so would indicate to Dick that he is far from the indolent playboy billionaire he's been pretending to be. On the other hand, Bruce couldn't just sit there—so ultimately, he does break free, and then he tells Dick who he really is.

That's how it went in our first draft, anyway. Then new leadership came in at DC, along with a new writer, Alan Heinberg. Out went our complicated story structure, which had the Joker acting as Two-Face's unwitting pawn, and gone, too, was the method of the reveal of Bruce's secret identity. Instead of it being caused by an admittedly convenient emergency, Bruce would now take pity on Dick, who is angry, frustrated and uncertain about his future—just as Bruce had been years earlier. Bruce is worried that Dick will do something rash, so he decides to offer Dick a way to save himself. It's the same route Bruce took: becoming a masked vigilante.

On stage, the scene played almost like a coming out story. It was as if an older gay man had come to realize a younger person is going through some of the same anguish he went through in his own youth. He talks to the confused boy about his own youthful confusion, and how he was finally able to find a satisfying existence for himself. So, instead of backing away from the implications that Dr. Wertham had written about, Heinberg embraced them and was able to turn the secret identity reveal into something that finally made emotional sense...

...at least for those in the arena who could see and hear it. Remember, this profoundly intimate moment was presented in a huge indoor arena; the scene hadn't made any impression at all on me the first two times I saw the show, and it wasn't until the third time, when I was sitting very close to the stage, that I finally got it.

Would children sitting as close as I was make the same inferences? I doubt it. Too adult. But not a huge loss for them, because, even if subtleties like that skipped over the heads of these lucky kids, the show's elaborate stagecraft certainly wouldn't have been wasted on them. And I'll wager that at least a few of the kids who sat close to the stage have become lifelong theatergoers thanks to that experience.

But what about the ones whose parents could only afford upper-level seats? They might have looked down on the spectacle that was unfolding so far below them and compared it unfavorably to seeing a movie. And those parents might've also been thinking about the hefty price they paid for this.

The high ticket prices—even for the so-called cheap seats—were unfortunate, but unavoidable; the *Batman Live* production posed huge logistical challenges: a big cast, a large support crew and lots of props to move around, including a gigantic video screen, an electric Batmobile (which was never intended to travel more than a few feet across the stage) and also, the Joker's preferred mode of transportation, a hot air balloon. Imagine having to truck all that material and all those people from one city to another every week. Then imagine the cost of housing and feeding all those people. Add to that the rental fees for the arenas, and you've got a backbreaking weekly nut.

The show had traveled around Europe before opening on the West Coast, and the plan was to sweep across the country to New York and then head off to Asia. But with show after show playing in front of audiences no larger than the one I first saw it with, *Batman Live* finally gave up the ghost somewhere in the Midwest. Nick Grace had been paying us tiny per-performance fees, but when the total amount got up to around two-thirds of what we'd agreed to as a minimum script fee, he simply stopped paying us. I couldn't blame him; I actually felt sorry for him. He was a huge Batman fan, and the Caped Crusader (and his many minions) had let him down quite grievously.

Informal postmortems suggested that the show hadn't been adequately promoted. A few billboards and some free spots on local television channels weren't enough, some said. But if you have a product that people really, really want, they'll find their way to it, making advertising all but irrelevant. That's why you never see ads for cocaine or crystal meth.

I'll always believe that the seeds for this disaster were planted at that very first meeting in New York, when the needs of the arena show medium were so quickly brushed aside. I still feel guilty for not having fought harder, but the thinking in the room seemed to be that with the word "Batman" in the title, there was no way we could go wrong. But we did, and *Batman Live* turned out to be the kind of disaster not even an Irwin Allen could have saved.

STAN BERKOWITZ

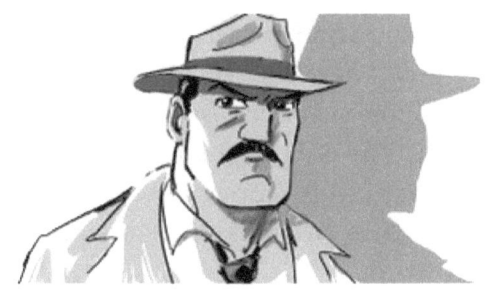

CHAPTER THIRTEEN
REGRETS

Teagan hadn't been living with me very long when she heard a sound she'd never heard me make before. She was in the bedroom, I was in the living room, and she couldn't tell if it was a cry of surprise, a whoop for a touchdown I'd seen on TV, or maybe I was in some kind of distress. She hurried into the living room and found me on the couch, staring at a copy of *Variety*... that was turned to the obituary page. And that unfamiliar sound she'd heard? It was one of sheer, unfettered joy.

The sky was a little bluer the rest of that day, the clouds whiter, and the sun seemed to shine just a bit brighter. But as night fell, my ecstasy was tempered by something else. Regret.

I don't find the dictionary definitions of the word "regret" terribly satisfying: "A sense of loss, disappointment or dissatisfaction." Kind of vague, I think. I'm only slightly more comfortable with "a feeling of sorrow or remorse for a fault," so maybe an example or two will clarify my personal definition of the word.

Let's say you wanted to write a novel but you didn't think the public would care about anything you had to say, so you never wrote it. Years later, a novel comes out that's similar to the one you wanted to write, and it's a big hit. That feeling you'd have would be what I'd call regret. On the other hand, let's say you do write that novel, but nobody reads it. That would certainly be a disappointment, but not necessarily a regret. Not unless you were pretty sure no one would read the thing before you started writing it, but you wrote it anyway.

To me, it's not a genuine, painful regret unless you second-guess yourself, and then later, you realize you shouldn't have. Or maybe you willfully ignore something crucial, and you eventually realize you should have known better. That's what hit me just a few hours after I saw that obit in *Variety*.

Seven years before the obit ran, I was working on a show called *The New Mike Hammer*, and I met Hammer's creator, Mickey Spillane. We spoke only briefly, but he struck me as one of the happiest people I'd ever met. And why shouldn't he have been? Before he was thirty, he'd become one of the world's most commercially successful authors.

His creation, Mike Hammer, was viewed by many as his alter ego (Spillane actually portrayed Hammer in a movie called *The Girl Hunters*), yet Hammer, even when played by Spillane, seemed like the author's polar opposite. Hammer made his living as a private detective, but he was more like the brutes and thugs who appeared as supporting characters in the mystery stories of earlier, comparatively more genteel writers like Dashiell Hammett and Raymond Chandler. In Spillane's stories, the aptly named Hammer would bull his way through his cases, take sadistic beatings, pay them back with interest, and along the way, he'd bed lots of beautiful women. At the end of the books, Hammer would show unexpected (and unlikely) intellect by quickly unraveling the whole complicated mystery.

The secret to Spillane's early success wasn't much of a mystery. His Hammer novels were the sexiest, most violent books that could be bought over the counter during the buttoned-down late '40s and 1950s. Like a stripper with pasties glued over her nipples, Spillane's books just barely slid past the censors. The *Hammer* movies of that era were a different story, because the movies' censor boards were a lot stricter than book censors. The movies could never be as daring as the books, so, with the exception of 1955's *Kiss Me Deadly*, which is generally considered a late noir masterpiece, neither the Mike Hammer movies nor a 1958 Hammer TV series made the kind of pop culture splash the books made. By the time Mickey Spillane put on the Hammer trench coat for 1963's *Girl Hunters*, hard-boiled detectives were old hat, or maybe, old fedora. They'd been supplanted on book racks and movie screens by a certain British secret agent.

Undeterred, Spillane continued to write, and the early '80s saw yet another incarnation of his signature detective. This time it was a CBS TV series, and Hammer was played by Stacy Keach, one of the most versatile actors to take on the role.

The show's executive producer was a former publicist and personal manager named Jay Bernstein, who caught the show business bug early, as a self-described lonely fat kid who found a refuge at the movies. He was a devoted film noir fan, but he knew that Hammer would have to be updated for the 1980s, and that meant transforming the character into a deliberate anachronism, an old-fashioned tough guy in a world of newly sensitive, politically correct males. Jay wanted Hammer to be the same guy he'd always been, but he'd be living in a world that had changed around him.

One thing that hadn't changed, at least according to Jay and the show's bible, was the fair sex; they were still falling at Hammer's feet—more so now than ever, the scripts insisted, because so many modern men were so wimpy. The writers were encouraged—actually, *ordered* by Bernstein—to write into every episode at least four girls—nicknamed Hammerettes--who'd run into Mike during the course of the stories, make a suggestive remark or two to him, then disappear. Not terribly realistic, given that Keach was by then a middle-aged man in a 1940's trench coat and, yes, a fedora, but it helped make the show lighter and a little more fun than the dark, brutal stuff that Spillane wrote.

The fun was interrupted just before Christmas of 1984, when Keach was given a six-month prison sentence in England for cocaine possession. Unprepared for the immediacy of the sentence (and by the Brits' utter lack of deference for someone who wasn't just a famous actor but also an individual upon whom over a hundred jobs depended), Bernstein scrambled to find a work-around. Cast a new Hammer, perhaps? Bring in a heretofore unknown Hammer brother for a few episodes? Or maybe focus on the show's supporting characters as they searched for a missing Mike? None of the alternatives sounded very appealing, so the studio sent the whole crew home. That included me -- just three weeks after I'd abruptly quit my years-long day job for this one.

The indefatigable Bernstein immediately began to lay out a strategy for getting his show back on the air, and very soon, he was able to convince CBS and the studio -- Columbia—to make a two-hour Hammer

TV movie that would begin shooting as soon as Keach got back from England. If the movie got good ratings, the series would be set to return in the fall of '86. And that's exactly what happened.

This time though, the series would be run as a tighter, more disciplined ship. Jay was an extraordinary salesman, and the studio needed good salesmen to sell their shows to the networks. (Despite the studio being called Columbia Pictures TV and Hammer's network being the Columbia Broadcasting System, they were separate entities.) But once Jay sold a show to the network and stepped into the executive producer role, there were some problems. For one, Jay had a hair-trigger temper, and for another, he didn't run a particularly tight ship, as evidenced by his star's catastrophic six-month absence, and also by an abnormally high turnover among the show's writing staff.

As a mere story editor, I wasn't in on the studio's and the network's personnel discussions, but in retrospect it's pretty easy to see that they both wanted a counterweight to Jay to head the writing staff — to be showrunner, though it wasn't called that in those days. They wanted a seasoned pro who'd make the trains run on schedule. Someone who'd keep a steady hand on the tiller, no matter what Jay did, or didn't do. So they brought in an Old Pro.

This particular Old Pro had started out writing radio dramas, transitioned to movies in the 1950s and got an Oscar nomination for his very first feature credit. After that, there were a couple of big hit TV shows, but then, from the late '60s onward, not so much. Just some TV movies and series that didn't get anywhere near the attention his earlier ones got. This track record, plus his advanced age—sixty-three— made him an unlikely candidate for showrunner, but early in 1986, a two-part TV movie he'd written had gotten good notices and ratings, so he was back in the game. And judging by his appearance, he was more than ready to play it again. A tall man with military posture, he looked like he spent hours a day on a rowing machine. He resembled a 1950s tough-guy actor named Robert Ryan—except the Old Pro wore thick glasses and used a dye that turned his thinning hair matte black outdoors... and purple indoors.

A showrunner's first duty is to turn out scripts. For a series debuting in October, the writing staff is usually assembled by Memorial Day, with shooting set to begin in July or August. That gives the writers a two-month head-start on production, which gobbles up scripts faster than they can be written.

The first sign of trouble on *Hammer* that season was that the Old Pro didn't bring any writers with him; he'd been doing TV movies so long, he no longer knew any staff writers with TV series experience. So he made do with three of us who'd been on the show during earlier seasons: a former dentist, an ex-sitcom writer and me. The second sign of trouble was that the

Old Pro hated most of the episode ideas that were being pitched by the elderly freelancers he'd invited in.

Just four years after this, I would find myself in a position similar to the Old Pro's on a different show, and the only solution I could think of was to do as much writing as I could myself. Whether it was outlining stories, writing scripts or rewriting them, I was where the buck stopped. But the Old Pro didn't see his responsibilities that way; instead, he decided that I was the problem.

If you happen to know me, I must assure you I wasn't like this back then. I was only a beginning writer with just one produced TV script and a season's experience as a staff writer. I'd hoped to sit quietly at the feet of the master and learn from him, but the Old Pro wasn't having that. Just two weeks in, before I or anyone else had written so much as a word, and all we were doing was listening to pitches from freelancers, the Old Pro came into my office, put his foot on my desk and told me it wasn't going to work out.

I was stunned, of course. I wondered what I had or hadn't done to deserve that, but he wasn't forthcoming. I just wasn't going to work out, period. Normally in a situation like that, the writer will then sit quietly in his office for the remainder of his contract (in my case, that would have been eighteen more weeks), so what the Old Pro told me might have been considered a courtesy in a way: he was letting me know he wouldn't renew my contract at the end of my guaranteed period, so if I had an opportunity elsewhere, I should take it. But I didn't have any other opportunities just then, and I would soon see that courtesy was the last thing the Old Pro cared about.

A few days later, he came back into my office, put his foot on my desk again and told me he'd changed his mind and that it would work out after all. Then, a few days after that, he told me he'd changed his mind yet again, and he was once again believed it wouldn't work out. He wanted me to leave... right then and there.

But there was a problem with that: he hadn't hired me. I'd been brought in by his boss -- Jay—and I'd signed a contract with the studio, so the Old Pro didn't have the power to fire me. That made him mad, and as the days passed, he got madder and madder. It soon became a power struggle between him and the studio, and there was a lot at stake for him: if they wouldn't let him fire a mere story editor, how could he hope to have the studio's support when he needed to stand up to the actors, directors, or Jay, who wasn't particularly pleased with his loss of influence over the scripts?

The Old Pro hated the outline I wrote, re-wrote it himself, then hated the one act of the teleplay he allowed me to write. Writers, especially ones who are just starting out, tend to go over every line they write, asking themselves if it's good enough. It's a key vulnerability, and to just tell a writer his stuff isn't good, without elaborating, is confirmation of his worst fear. And an Old Pro would certainly have known this, having once had those doubts himself, and, quite possibly, still having them.

In the scheme of things, the Old Pro's problem with me was small stuff, but the big stuff wasn't going well, either. With the first day of shooting looming, the Old Pro's four-man literary department had scrapped a bunch of the outlines the elderly freelancers wrote, and had generated just one finished script, which was not without its problems. Our effusive former dentist's script was a searing indictment of social injustice — or would've been, had we been living in 1946. The story hinged on a wealthy businessman who was adamant in his belief that his right-hand man wasn't good enough to marry his daughter.

"So, this right-hand man, he's Black or Mexican or Jewish? Or maybe a Democrat?" I asked the dentist, who was always at his most effusive when talking about his own work.

"No, he's just from a different social class, that's all," he replied.

Yeah, right. In America. In 1986. Later, upon reflection, the dentist decided to compromise and give the right-hand man a different surname. An Armenian one.

To bolster his small writing staff, which still consisted of just the dentist, me and the sitcom writer (whom the Old Pro also openly detested), the Old Pro eventually added an even Older Pro—a prolific actor, director and writer whose resume went all the way back to pre-World War II radio and who had been a mentor to the Old Pro. But this Older Pro was destined to spend his days at the studio writing very long critiques of the outlines that were being turned in by the freelancers, only to have the Old Pro ignore everything he wrote.

It was looking like what had happened to the show before—an untimely (and expensive) halt in production—was going to happen again. And this time, it wouldn't be because of a jail sentence; blame would fall squarely on the broad shoulders of the Old Pro. As best as I could tell, the Old Pro was now hoping to generate the scripts as close as possible to their production dates, so the studio and the network would have no choice but to approve them, because if they didn't, there would come that halt in production.

As you would imagine, the studio wasn't happy about this. The tight ship they expected the Old Pro to run was looking loose and in danger of sinking, so the pressure was building on the Old Pro from all directions. Eight weeks in, the Old Pro responded the only way he could think of: by throwing a fit and ordering me out of my office. He didn't have the power to do that, but he effectively made it impossible for me to stay there.

By leaving the office, I might have been considered in breach of my contract, which still had twelve more weeks to go, but the studio executives, whom I'd known for two years, were, of course, aware of what was going on with the Old Pro, and they and my agents quickly set up an interview for me on another of the studio's shows. The interview went well and just a week after the Old Pro put his foot on my desk for the last time, I was writing for that new show. As it turned out, I would be on this show far beyond my original contract—almost two more years. I'd eventually earn a co-producer title, and I made lifelong friends there, too.

But you're probably wondering what happened to the Old Pro, whose suite of offices was just across a small courtyard from my new office. As soon as I was gone, he hired a replacement for me: the dentist's son, who'd come ill-prepared to a pitch meeting I'd attended a few weeks earlier. He'd offered next to nothing, but was given an assignment anyway. And then he got my job. Funny how things work when family is involved. Then, as production began, the Old Pro walked into a series of buzz saws.

The first came in the form of a diminutive man in his late sixties named Seymour Friedman. Seymour, as everyone at the studio called him, had been there for decades. He was the man who questioned a production office if a secretary ordered one more box of Kleenex than she ordered the previous month. But his purview wasn't just trivial expenses; he was also the man you'd call if your lead actress was having a nervous breakdown and wouldn't come out of her trailer. Or if your star was facing a jail sentence in England.

Seymour couldn't solve every problem that popped up, but if he couldn't, the problem was written off as unsolvable. He'd started as an assistant director in the 1940s, graduated to directing B-pictures, and then he became one of the studio's vice-presidents. He could not have been pleased by the scarcity of Hammer scripts, because when the studio's various production departments don't have plenty of time to prepare for episodes, the chances of going over budget increase. And to Seymour, every penny the studio wasted was like a drop of his own blood.

Then there was Stacy Keach. During shooting, he would normally keep the sitcom writer with him in his trailer, and together they would revise that day's scenes, usually with an eye toward adding some humor. The next day, when the dailies screened, the writing staff would wonder what happened to the scenes they'd spent weeks writing. But there was nothing they could do. Everyone had seen what happened when Stacy was taken out of the picture: there was no picture. There was nothing the Old Pro could have done about it, either — angry as that might have made him.

In contrast, things were going relatively smoothly on my new show in the weeks after I left *Hammer*. Our only hindrance was a writer-producer I'll call Howard, who was much better at telling us why stories wouldn't work than at helping to make them work. Our new supervising producer/showrunner was trying to figure out what to do about Howard when he got a call from one of the Columbia execs, a friend of his since high school. The exec had some gossip about the Old Pro: facing restiveness, if not outright rebellion almost everywhere he looked, the Old Pro had put his foot down, figuratively, this time. He told the studio exec that from now on, it had to be his way or the highway.

Much to the Old Pro's surprise, the executive took him up on his ultimatum, telling him he wasn't going to be given his way, so now he needed to leave the studio. That day.

The Old Pro was taken aback, as are most people who overplay their hand. He quickly backtracked, said he didn't mean it, was still ready and able to do his job, etc. etc., but the executive wasn't having any of it; this would be the Old Pro's last day at the studio. Everyone there—except the dentist and his son—had had enough of him.

My new supervising producer listened sympathetically to this, then told his old friend, "Now I know why you called."

"You do?"

"You want to take Howard from me, and use him to replace [the Old Pro]. But I'm not going to let you have him."

"I can have him if I want him," the exec said, this undoubtedly being the first time the exec considered "stealing" Howard.

"You can't have him," the supervising producer insisted.

I imagine it went on that way for a while, like Br'er Rabbit and the briar patch or Tom Sawyer and the fence that needed to be painted. And then, just a day or two after that conversation, Howard said his goodbyes to us. He'd gotten what he considered a well-deserved promotion to a co-supervising producer role on the *Hammer* show. We were all very happy for him.

After that, I didn't pay close attention to the Old Pro's fortunes. His firing of me looked bad on my resume, but his own behavior at the studio discredited him so thoroughly, who would now care what he thought about me or anyone else? What little of the stain on me that might have remained was washed away the following summer, after what I imagine were some legal maneuverings that had to do with his abrupt departure from *Hammer*.

CBS gave him another show to run, but once again, there was an early departure, and this time, the Old Pro couldn't blame an erratic executive producer or a skinflint studio. So, he was out for good and so was the dentist, whom the Old Pro had brought along with him to this other studio. Back at Columbia, a line producer who had worked briefly for the Old Pro danced an exuberant jig when he heard what happened to his old nemesis.

During the seemingly endless eight weeks I worked for the Old Pro, I was never able to figure out why he hated me so much that he couldn't even stand to have me quietly sit out my contract. My best guess at the time was some kind of mental illness, and only later did it occur to me that he might have thought I was spying on him. A young writer with a thin résumé, quietly watching everything he did? Sounds like I might have been spying on him for Jay. After all, it'd been Jay who hired me. It seems paranoid, but it wasn't.

If my guess is correct, it means the Old Pro had read Jay quite astutely. I would learn later that asking his employees to spy on other employees was exactly the sort of thing Jay did, although in this case, he hadn't bothered to ask that of me—largely because he didn't need a spy to know that the Old Pro's script department wasn't generating scripts, just as you wouldn't need an inside man at the electric plant to know there'd been a power failure.

The sitcom writer had a different take: "[The Old Pro] was insecure, scared," he told me, and the more I thought about it, the more sense that made. Imagine if you'd had enormous early success, so much that even twenty or thirty years later, people fondly remembered the shows you worked on. And then you were asked to re-create that success. Sure, the show you'd make would be competent, even good, but would it be a hit? That's one thing no one, not even an Old Pro, can guarantee.

And he had to know that. If the show flops, what will happen to his cherished legacy? So, out of fear, was he lashing out at everyone around him, except, of course, the dentist, who seemed to always be brimming with enthusiasm? That enthusiasm was a straw the Old Pro could grasp as his own confidence flagged.

Should I have offered the Old Pro straws of my own? Sucked up to him, tried to make him feel more secure? It might have helped me, but it wouldn't have done any good for the show. And besides, I've never been much good at that particular kind of dishonesty. Nor have I wanted to be.

These days, I wonder if the Old Pro's insecurity led to an unconscious desire to fail. To quit or be fired before the public could ever have its say on whether he still had his finger on its pulse. Possible, even likely. But shouldn't he have been aware of this? Sure, self-analysis wasn't a big factor in the lives of the

World War II generation, but when protection of one ego threatened the livelihoods of so many other people, maybe a little time on an analyst's couch wouldn't have been such a bad idea.

Early on *Hammer*, the Old Pro bragged about not needing money, saying he was working because he enjoyed "the action." But there were a lot of people on the show who were not set for life, and who did need the money. "Action" was not foremost among *their* motivations.

Wait, wasn't this chapter supposed to be about regrets? Could mine be that I chose not to "happen" to be in our shared courtyard when the Old Pro carried out a cardboard box with his papers and made his way to his big Mercedes for the final time? I'll confess, I would have liked to watch that, and I would have especially liked it if the Old Pro had seen me watching him. But doing that would have made my colleagues on my new show question my maturity, which was something I was not ready to let them do so early in our relationship.

No, my regret revolved around a realization that hit me the day I read that the Old Pro had suddenly dropped dead on a tennis court, almost seven years after the eight miserable weeks I'd worked for him. Driving into the studio's parking lot during those weeks, I would pray that the Old Pro's Mercedes wouldn't be there.

BEYOND THE BAT

I wasn't really praying, of course. It was more like a gambler fervently wishing his number would come up on a roulette wheel. All I wanted at that point was to sit out the remainder of my twenty weeks, then find a new career. For that to happen, the Old Pro would have to not show up for a while.

"Come on, God, let him be in an accident this morning. Give him a broken leg. Or maybe a heart attack or a stroke that'll keep him in bed and away from the office until my twenty weeks are up. Please, God," I would mutter, without a trace of the piety my ancestors had when they beseeched the white-bearded man in the sky.

But my faithlessness was shaken by the news of the Old Pro's death, and it was the way the news arrived that started the shaking. The copy of *Variety* that had the Old Pro's obit wasn't something I picked up at a newsstand; I'd found it on the lawn of our triplex, and it was the only time a copy of the magazine ever showed up there. Yet there it was, with the Old Pro's obit waiting to send me into ecstasy. How had that particular issue, and *only* that one, gotten there? And why? Could it have been... providence?

For just a moment or two, it felt as if the God from the Old Testament, the one who dispensed justice brutally and often excessively (though in this case, a bit tardily), still answered prayers, even ones that were uttered casually and without any expectation they'd be answered.

So, for that brief moment of belief, I regretted something. I regretted that I hadn't prayed for an even worse fate for the Old Pro. Death for sure, but something far more protracted than a sudden heart attack. Something that would have given him plenty of time to marinate in his own regrets. And if it turned out he didn't have any, at least he would have spent many, many months in excruciating physical pain.

God willing, of course.

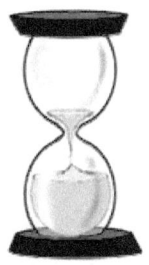

CHRONOLOGY

You've no doubt noticed that the preceding essays jump all over the time/space continuum. That was always the plan, because what I wanted to say with the essays was, and is, more important than the specific details of my life, where chance plays as big a role as it probably does in yours.

Still, I figured some readers wouldn't be able to loosen their grip on the concept of cause-and-effect (I probably wouldn't either, if this were someone else's book), so here's everything in chronological order:

1949: Born. My parents were living in a small apartment on Arnaz Drive in Beverly Hills, just down the street from Stanley Drive. I wonder how they came up with a name for me.

1955: I start first grade in California's suburban San Fernando Valley and almost immediately develop an intense mistrust of authority figures. This will serve me well when I start to write stories for superhero vigilantes like Batman and Spider-Man. You can read all about this in *The Green Group* chapter, if you haven't already.

1963: Junior high school in Reseda, California. Improbably enough, I get my start in home movies as an actor. I'm working for a fourteen-year-old friend who'd just seen *Lawrence of Arabia* and wanted to restage the opening's motorcycle crash. Since I'd just gotten a used Schwinn ten-speed bicycle—a model that happened to look slightly less unlike a motorcycle than his other friends' bikes—I got the Peter O'Toole role.

In a heavy turtleneck sweater and plastic goggles that slowly filled with sweat on a hot afternoon, I quickly realized that what I really wanted to do was direct. And, with my parents' 8mm Brownie home movie camera in hand, that's what I soon started doing. But I stopped for a while at age 16. This next item had something to do with it...

1966: I start attending UCLA part-time, at the same time as I begin my senior year of high school. I would soon be making movies again, but they'd look a lot different from the childish ones I made in my early teens. (See the *Saying Something* chapter.)

1968: I start writing movie reviews for UCLA's student newspaper, the *Daily Bruin*.

1969: I make a Project One student film (the *Saying Something* chapter again), and I'm still writing for the *Daily Bruin*. At the end of the year, I interview X-rated filmmaker Russ Meyer on the set of his first major studio production, *Beyond the Valley of the Dolls*.

1970: I write and direct *Ass* (*Saying Something*), and I also become editor of one of the *Daily Bruin*'s two entertainment sections.

1971: I finish my Project Two (*Ars Longa Vita Brevis*—the *Saying Something* chapter yet again), get my BA in film production and begin grad school, also at UCLA. In two years, I'll have an MFA certificate in screenwriting, something no prospective employer will ever ask to see.

1971: I write a short review of an obscure Burt Lancaster film, *Lawman*, for a Los Angeles-based magazine called *Coast FM and Fine Arts*. It's the first time I'm paid to write something. I get $15. Forty-nine years later, a Chinese company contacts me via Linked In to offer me work writing educational material… at that very same rate, not even adjusted for inflation.

1973: I get my first script agent. Nothing comes of it.

1973: I get my MFA in screenwriting and start a part-time job for Russ Meyer, inspecting theatrical prints of his old films for damage—frame by frame—and re-splicing them when necessary. My father makes a joke about the guy who sweeps up after the circus's elephants; at least he's in show business!

1974: All that splicing pays off! Russ hires me to be a grip on the very small and hard-working crew of his X-rated film-a-clef, *The Supervixens*. Twelve weeks later, I am out of work.

1974: Continuing to write spec scripts, I go to work for a small post-production company owned by a former teacher of mine from UCLA. I'm writing narrations for pre-existing educational films, and the words have to be simple and articulated very clearly by the narrators, because the audience for these things is people who are hearing-impaired. What'll be next? Writing porn movies for people who don't see very well?

1975: I get a new agent. Nothing comes of this, either. So, I keep working at the post-production company.

1976: With my college friend and collaborator David Lees, I finally sell a story to a fledgling film company... without the help of our alleged agent, who tells us we could make as much money working as waiters as we would if we accepted the company's meager offer. We accept the offer anyway and turn the story into a full script. But when we see the rewritten version, we tell the producer we only want credit for the original story.

The film was called *Acapulco Gold*, it played in one theater in Los Angeles for one week at the end 1976, and then later throughout the city as the bottom half of a double bill... with a Cheech and Chong movie, to no one's surprise.

1977: I go back to the post-production company. But I keep writing spec scripts and doing freelance journalism.

1977. David and I get an assignment from Larry Flynt's *Chic* magazine, a sister publication to his *Hustler* Magazine. Improbably, they want us to do an article about auteur filmmaker Robert Altman. Even more improbably, this article will lead to more work from other publications...

1978: Like the *Los Angeles Times*'s entertainment section. I'm getting busier, but I'm not going to give up my day job at the post-production house, which has morphed into a film restoration company. So now I'm a part-time film restorer and a part-time journalist, the latter of which will eventually lead to...

1979: ...Vintage Books, a division of Random House, offering to pay David and me to put together a compilation of our film journalism under the title *The Movie Business: A Primer*. Sounds easy, right? It's not. The editor asks for so much new material, we have to spend the next year researching and writing.

1981: The book comes out. It goes into a second printing fairly quickly—but I still won't quit my day job. So, I keep writing spec scripts, and somewhere around here I acquire a new literary agent. (A literary agent -- at least in L.A.—represents scripts and screenwriters, while our Random House deal was handled by a book agent, which is an entirely different profession.) This newest literary agent doesn't lead anywhere, either.

1982–1983: More spec scripts, more film journalism, and still working at my day job. Will it always be like this?

1984, February: I get a call from a college friend inviting me to pitch a story idea for Universal's *Knight Rider*. They don't use my idea, but they pay me anyway—so I keep my day job.

1984, June: I get yet another agent. This time, a lot happens.

1984, Early December: After I show my two newest spec scripts to everyone I know, a friend who'd become a producer at Columbia Pictures TV offers me a staff writer position on the new *Mike Hammer* TV series. But I'd have to quit my day job in order to take it. I think about it for less time than it'll take you to finish this sentence.

1984, Late December: Maybe I should have thought about it a little longer. With our Mike Hammer, Stacy Keach, suddenly jailed in England on drug charges, Columbia sends everyone home, just in time for Christmas. I start making phone calls.

1985, January: One of my calls is answered at 20th Century Fox, and I am immediately hired to write an episode of a show called *Cover Up*. Whew!

1985, June: I get a job as a staff writer on *TJ Hooker*. (See the *Dammit Hooker, She Was My Niece!* chapter).

1985, Late: A mutual friend introduces me to Teagan Clive, whom I'll eventually marry. Keep reading to see how long it takes me to work up the courage to ask her to lunch.

1986–1988: *TJ Hooker* ends, but *Mike Hammer* is reborn. Unfortunately for me, the new boss is not the same as the old boss, and this one hates me. (See *Regrets* chapter). Columbia graciously reassigns me to a new show, *Houston Knights*. I keep my head low, and as a result, I'm the only member of the writing staff whose name appears at the end of all 31 episodes.

1988: The Writers' Guild goes out on a long strike, after which I write a story for *Star Trek, The Next Generation*, which never makes it to the script stage. But...

1989: ...one of *The Next Generation*'s producers liked the outline I wrote enough to hire me to write scripts for updated reboots of *Dragnet* and *Adam 12*.

1990: As those freelance assignments run out, I'm hired as writer–producer for season three (and later, season four) of the *Adventures of Superboy*. The downside: long hours and having to live in Orlando for a year. The upside: a life-changing amount of compensation... which gives me enough confidence to...

1992: ...finally ask Teagan to lunch. Things move swiftly from there, and our relationship will eventually turn out to be like ice cream: more vanilla than you'd expect, but enlivened by occasional rocky road.

1993: I work with a director I met on *Dragnet* to develop a script for a low budget feature. It gets made—eventually— and not without controversy (consider the title of the *Racism and Me* chapter).

1994: Teagan and I get married, and almost the minute we get back from our brief honeymoon, I go to work for Marvel Animation, Fox Kids and Stan Lee on a new *Spider-Man* animated series. (See the *When Things Go Well* chapter).

1995: My film school friend, "Lucky," dies suddenly. (See the *Playing the Odds* chapter).

1996: I switch over to Warners Animation as a writer and story editor for their new *Superman* series. (*When Things Go Well* again). Soon, we'll start making more episodes of Warners' classic *Batman* series.

1997: I take a brief hiatus from Warner Bros to go to work at Universal on Dick Wolf's live-action series, *Players*.

1998: Back to Warners for *Batman Beyond* and an Emmy for *The New Batman/Superman Adventures*. (See the *How to Win an Emmy* chapter).

1998: I find out that one of my unions' pensions isn't going to be what I assumed it would be, and I quickly become a union activist.

2001–2004: We win another Emmy, this time for *Batman Beyond*. Then it's on to *Static Shock*, and after that, the *Justice League* series. (See the *When Things Go Well...* chapter again).

2004: I quit Warners to work with some English people—and an ex-pat American, Gary Kurtz, who produced the first two *Star Wars* movies—on an animated Bible show called *Friends and Heroes*. (See the *Animating the Bible* chapter)

2005–2009: Back to Warners, this time as a freelancer writing for *The Batman*, as well as adapting the *Justice League: New Frontier* and *Batman/Superman: Public Enemies* features.

2009–2011: Some colleagues from *Friends and Heroes* recommend me for a job as story editor of a new animated superhero show called *THE 99*. Because some of our 99 superheroes come from predominantly Muslim countries, the *New York Post* issues their version of a fatwah against it—without ever seeing it—and as a result, the show's American cable outlet cancels it before even a single episode is aired.

And, as if to prove that you can't please all the people all the time, but you can certainly offend them all at once, *THE 99*'s creator is accused of blasphemy in Kuwait... where a charge like that can get you into way more trouble than a bad review. (See the *Half-Million Dollar Bowl of Soup* chapter)

2009: The Writers' Guild gives me its Animation Writing Award, most likely because I made sure that my fellow writers on *Friends and Heroes* and *THE 99* all got covered by Writers Guild contracts. (In animation, Writers' Guild coverage is not guaranteed, the way it is in live action.) The Guild's award ceremony felt like a memorial service, minus the corpse.

2010: I become one of the writers on the *Batman Live* arena show, and later, I nearly forget to include that credit on this list. (See the *Robin Problem* chapter)

2010 – 2015: Lots of freelance animation scripts: *Ben 10, G.I. Joe, Marvel's Superhero Squad, Avengers Assemble, Thunderbirds, Transformers, Justice League Action*, and some others you've probably never heard of.

2015 – 2019: Writing scripts for animation, graphic novels, and lots of travel for meetings and research: New York City (in a blizzard), Copenhagen, Berlin, Martha's Vineyard, San Francisco, San Diego, Saudi Arabia, Beirut, Paris, Vancouver, Miami, San Salvador, Beijing and southeast China. All on different airlines, so no frequent flyer miles.

2020: Covid-19 arrives, and the fun stops. Temporarily, I hope.

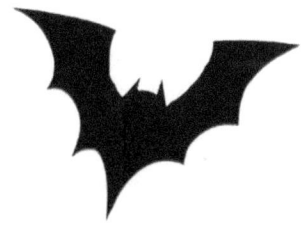

ACKNOWLEDGMENTS

I couldn't have written this book without the valuable feedback from these generous people, whom I'm listing in alphabetical order: Les Barnum, Maureen Foster, the late Phil Freshman, Kathryn Galán, Susan Jaskolka, David Lees, Debbie Reinberg, Evelyn Renold, Dan Riba, Richard Stayton, and Mia Walshaw.

Many, many thanks!

STAN BERKOWITZ

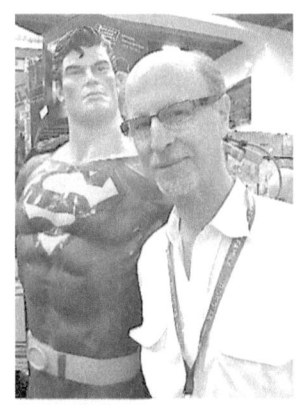

ABOUT THE AUTHOR

Stan Berkowitz started writing professionally in 1971 and hasn't stopped. He began with film reviews for *Coast* magazine, then started doing show business-related journalism for *Esquire*, *The Los Angeles Times*, *The New York Daily News* and many others. He co-authored a book, *The Movie Business: A Primer*, and then began a long career writing for television, first for police shows and then for superhero shows, both animated and live-action.

He's written for *Superman, Superboy, Batman, Batman, Batman Beyond, Spider-Man, Wonder Woman, Green Lantern, the Transformers, GI Joe, Ben 10, The Legion of Superheroes* and many, many others.

STAN BERKOWITZ

A graduate of UCLA's MFA screenwriting program, he's won two Emmys as well as the Writers Guild of America's Animation Writer Award. He continues to write scripts for TV animation and graphic novels.

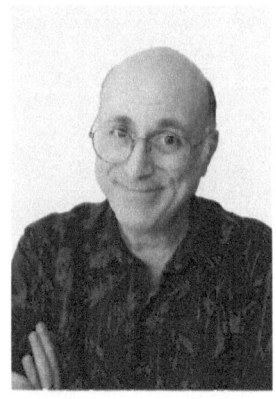

ABOUT THE ILLUSTRATOR

Dan Riba is a three-time Emmy winning animation director with over 35 years of industry experience. He is renowned for his significant contributions, especially in the realm of superhero animated series.

He is best known for his work as a director; however, he has also worked as a character designer, storyboard artist and assistant animator. His work has also earned him an Eisner Award. The Will Eisner Comic Industry Awards (Eisner Awards) are given for creative achievement in American comic books.

www.ingramcontent.com/pod-product-compliance
Lightning Source LLC
Chambersburg PA
CBHW020642220526
45464CB00001B/259